FROM SABBATH STO SUNDAY

The Attempt
to Change
God's Holy
Day...

FROM SABBATH TO SUNDAY

CARLYLE B. HAYNES

A Discussion of the Historical Aspects of the Sabbath Question,
Showing How, When, Why, and by Whom the Change Was
Made From the Seventh to the First Day of the Week

REVIEW AND HERALD PUBLISHING ASSOCIATION

Hagerstown, MD 21740

Contents

The Change in Sabbath Observance 7

The Bible Sabbath 13

Divine Authority for the Change Lacking 19

How, Why, and by Whom the Change Was
    Brought About 31

The Identical Seventh Day 49

The Change of the Calendar 65

The Position of Protestantism 75

Ancient Prophecies of Modern Sabbathkeeping 99

Completing an Arrested Reformation 112

Walking in the Light 123

Sabbathkeeping is inextricably bound up with the church and its services, for Sabbathkeeping means worship as well as rest.

The Change in Sabbath Observance

SOMEWHERE in the dim ages between the time of Christ and our time, the observance of the Sabbath has been changed from the seventh day of the week to the first day.

Certain it is that the command of God is for the sanctification and observance of the seventh day as the Sabbath. There can be no mistaking the meaning here. This is the command:

"Remember the sabbath day, to keep it holy. Six days shalt thou labour, and do all thy work: but the seventh day is the sabbath of the Lord thy God: in it thou shalt not do any work, thou, nor thy son, nor thy daughter, thy manservant, nor thy maidservant, nor thy cattle, nor thy stranger that is within thy gates: for in six days the Lord made heaven and earth, the sea, and all that in them is, and rested the seventh day: wherefore the Lord blessed the sabbath day, and hallowed it" (Exodus 20:8-11).

Equally certain it is that there is no other command given in the Holy Scriptures naming another or a different day. The Bible in its entirety, both Old and New Testaments, commands, upholds, defends, and teaches the observance of the seventh day as the Sabbath.

Just as certain is it that the various churches of Christian believers today, in every part of the world, with but few im-

F. R. GRUGER, ARTIST

The only divine law for Sabbath observance known among men was spoken with the other nine from Sinai's height by God Himself and delivered to Moses.

portant exceptions, uniformly observe the first day of the
week, and unite in defending its observance.

There appears, then, to be a discrepancy between the pres-
ent-day practice of the churches in the matter of Sabbathkeeping and the plain teaching of the Bible. This apparent
discrepancy has disturbed the minds of many, and created a
real need for accurate and reliable information regarding the
historical background of the change in Sabbath observance,
the time this change took place, and the reasons for making
the change. Therefore, it is proposed here to enter into a
study of this subject in the hope of providing information
that will enable every reader to arrive at such clear convictions
of truth and duty as will remove all doubt and confusion.

In such a study it will be necessary, of course, to inquire
into the origin of Sabbath observance, as well as to examine
the writings setting forth the history of the church and the reasons for the change of the day. We shall therefore be required to give careful consideration to the Bible account of
the establishment of the Sabbath among men, and the reasons
in the mind of God for commanding its observance in one
of His ten commandments.

The Law Spoken and Written by Jehovah

The only divine law for Sabbath observance known
among men is contained in the Bible, and has been quoted on
the preceding page. It should be pointed out that this commandment was spoken, with the other nine commandments,
by the mouth of Jehovah Himself.

"The Lord spake unto you out of the midst of the fire: ye
heard the voice of the words, but saw no similitude; only ye
heard a voice. And he declared unto you . . . ten commandments" (Deuteronomy 4:12, 13).

These commandments, including the Sabbath commandment, were written with God's own finger on enduring stone. "He wrote them upon two tables of stone" (Deuteronomy 4:13). "Two tables of testimonies, tables of stone, written with the finger of God" (Exodus 31:18).

This law is spoken of in the Scriptures as "right," "true," "good," and "perfect." "Thou camest down also upon Mount Sinai, and spakest with them from heaven, and gavest them right judgments, and true laws, good statutes and commandments" (Nehemiah 9:13). "The law of the Lord is perfect" (Psalm 19:7).

This law contains the whole duty of man.

Christ Did Not Change the Law

It was not the purpose of Christ to change, remove, destroy, or nullify any part of this law. "Think not that I am come to destroy the law, or the prophets: I am not come to destroy, but to fulfil" (Matthew 5:17).

Instead of discrediting the law, Christ came to make it honorable. "He will magnify the law, and make it honourable" (Isaiah 42:21).

Indeed, so far as the Sabbath is concerned, Christ observed it, with every other commandment. "As his custom was, he went into the synagogue on the sabbath day" (Luke 4:16).

As a matter of fact, faith in Christ, instead of setting the law aside, establishes and confirms it. "Do we then make void the law through faith? God forbid: yea, we establish the law" (Romans 3:31).

This law of God, containing the Sabbath commandment, is declared by Paul to be "spiritual," "holy," "just," and "good." "We know that the law is spiritual" (Romans 7:14).

"Wherefore the law is holy, and the commandment holy, and just, and good" (verse 12).

This law must be kept as a condition of eternal life. "Blessed are they that do his commandments, that they may have right to the tree of life, and may enter in through the gates into the city" (Revelation 22:14).

Indeed, it is the rule, or standard, by which the entire world will be judged. "So speak ye, and so do, as they that shall be judged by the law of liberty" (James 2:12).

The Law Remains in Force

It seems strange, therefore, that such an observance as the Sabbath should have been changed at all. The law of God still remains in force. That law requires the observance of the seventh day of the week. But that day is not now observed by the overwhelming majority of the professed people of God. Nevertheless, the law remains unchanged, is still in force, and is the standard of God's judgment.

Another day has been substituted for the day commanded. Where did that day come from? Why has it been substituted? Is its observance acceptable to God?

These are the questions to which we shall now address ourselves.

Jesus Christ, the Author of the Christian religion, is also the Author of the Sabbath. He brought it into existence when He created the world in six days and rested the seventh.

The Bible Sabbath

THE Author of the Sabbath is the Author of the Christian religion—Jesus Christ, the Son of God.

He it was who brought the world into existence, making it in six days. He it was who rested on the seventh day, and blessed that day, and made it holy. For the Son of God was and is the Creator. "All things were made by him."

"In the beginning was the Word, and the Word was with God, and the Word was God. The same was in the beginning with God. All things were made by him; and without him was not any thing made that was made" (John 1:1-3). "He was in the world, and the world was made by him, and the world knew him not" (verse 10). "The Word was made flesh, and dwelt among us, (and we beheld his glory, the glory as of the only begotten of the Father,) full of grace and truth" (verse 14).

"Who is the image of the invisible God, the firstborn of every creature: for by him were all things created, that are in heaven, and that are in earth, visible and invisible, whether they be thrones, or dominions, or principalities, or powers: all things were created by him" (Colossians 1:15, 16).

The time when He made the Sabbath, as we have already seen, was at the end of the Creation week. (Genesis 2:1-3.)

13

The way in which He made the Sabbath was by taking a day, the seventh day, and resting on it, blessing it, and sanctifying it.

The Sabbath a Day, Not an Institution

The material out of which He made the Sabbath was the seventh day. He took that day, and out of it made the Sabbath. The Sabbath is not something He placed on the day. It is the day itself. "The seventh *day* is the sabbath of the Lord thy God."

We are not commanded to "remember the *Sabbath,* to keep it holy." The command is, "Remember the sabbath *day,* to keep *it* [the day] holy." The Sabbath is not something apart from the day, which can be shifted about and perhaps placed on another day. It is the day itself, the seventh day.

We hear much today about a Sabbath *institution.* But the Bible never speaks of a Sabbath *institution.* It talks about the Sabbath *day.* There is no such thing as a Sabbath *institution* that was blessed and made holy for the benefit of humanity, apart from a day.

It was the *day* that was blessed and made holy; and it is the *day* that thus becomes the Sabbath.

The day that God blessed can never be taken from the Sabbath. The Sabbath can never be taken from the day that God blessed. These cannot be separated. They are inseparable because they are one.

The *seventh day* is the Sabbath; the Sabbath is the *seventh day.*

Jesus made the Sabbath for the entire human race, not for one section or one nation. "The sabbath was made for man" (Mark 2:27).

The Sabbath of Eternal Duration

God made the Sabbath for all time. It was not designed to be of temporary duration, but of eternal. The time will never come when the seventh day is not the blessed, holy rest day of God. "All his commandments are sure. They stand fast for ever and ever" (Psalm 111:7, 8).

Even in the new earth the blessed seventh-day Sabbath will be observed by the nations of the saved. "It shall come to pass, that . . . from one sabbath to another, shall all flesh come to worship before me, saith the Lord" (Isaiah 66:23).

The reason why God commanded men to observe the Sabbath day is: "For in six days the Lord made heaven and earth, the sea, and all that in them is, and rested the seventh day: wherefore the Lord blessed the sabbath day, and hallowed it" (Exodus 20:11).

The Sabbath, therefore, is a memorial of the creation of the earth in six literal days, and God has established it as a sign of His creative power. Through the observance of it God purposed that man should always keep Him in remembrance as the true and only God, the Creator of all things.

A Sign of Sanctification

The creative power of God was put forth the second time in the work of redemption, which is in reality a new creation. The Sabbath as a memorial of creative power thus becomes a memorial of our salvation in Christ. It was definitely set forth as a sign of sanctification. "I gave them my sabbaths, to be a sign between me and them, that they might know that I am the Lord that sanctify them" (Ezekiel 20:12).

As Christ is the one who sanctifies His people, the Sabbath therefore becomes a sign of what Christ is to the believer.

It is a memorial of our rest in Him, our rest from sin, of the completion of His work of full salvation in us. As such a memorial it is to endure forever.

It is Jesus who saves from sin. This salvation from sin is the actual working in us of the creative power of God. Only through that power, brought to sinners by the Holy Spirit, can sin be overcome in human flesh, and man enter into the rest of faith. It is Jesus who gives this rest.

"Come unto me, all ye that labour and are heavy laden, and *I will give you rest*" (Matthew 11:28).

A Sign of Deliverance From Sin

The sign of that creative power of Christ is the Sabbath. "Sabbath" means rest. It was given not merely for physical rest but as a sign of spiritual rest and deliverance from sin. Hence he who keeps the Sabbath understandingly has entered into the rest of God, and "he that is entered into his rest, he also hath ceased from his own works, as God did from his" (Hebrews 4:10).

In this way the Sabbath becomes to the believer in Christ a symbol of all that the gospel contains for him in Christ.

Beginning and Ending of the Sabbath

The Sabbath begins at sunset and ends at sunset. The Bible method of reckoning days is not from midnight to midnight, but from sunset to sunset. When the sun goes down, the day is ended and a new day begins. The evening is the beginning of the day. "The evening and the morning were the first day" (Genesis 1:5). That is, the evening, or dark part of the day, comes first, and is followed by the morning, or light part.

The instruction of God is, "From even unto even, shall ye celebrate your sabbath" (Leviticus 23:32).

The "even" begins at sunset. "At even, at the going down of the sun" (Deuteronomy 16:6). "At even, when the sun did set" (Mark 1:32).

When, therefore, the sun goes down on the evening of the sixth day of the week, that marks the beginning of God's Sabbath. Friday night at sunset is the dividing line between secular and sacred time. The hours between sunset Friday night and sunset Saturday night are holy time. "The Lord *blessed* the sabbath day, and *hallowed* it" (Exodus 20:11).

It is this sacred time that we are commanded to "remember" in order "to keep it holy." God *made* it holy; He commands man to *keep* it holy.

The Purpose of Sabbathkeeping

To keep the Sabbath holy is to use it for the purpose for which it was appointed. It was designed to be a day for public worship as well as private devotion. "The seventh day is the sabbath of rest, *a holy convocation*" (Leviticus 23:3). We have the example of Christ Himself in attending public worship on the Sabbath. "As his custom was, he went into the synagogue on the sabbath day" (Luke 4:16).

Preparation for proper Sabbathkeeping includes the cooking of food and the preparation of all other things that may be needful in order to be ready to cease from secular, earthly employment when the Sabbath is beginning, and devote ourselves to sacred, heavenly things (Exodus 16:22, 23; Luke 23:54).

The Sabbath is not a day for ordinary labor, for idleness, for amusement. It is for rest, spiritual as well as physical; for meditation; for worship, private as well as public; for holy joy; and for mutual helpfulness. It was designed to be the happiest, brightest, and best day of all the seven.

Fundamental to Edenic Ideals

It is one of two survivals of Edenic life that have persisted since the Fall, the other being the marriage institution, and it is, therefore, fundamental to Edenic ideals. This day of rest occurs weekly, in order to keep always before us the fact of God's rest at the close of Creation week. We are to remember God every day, but the Sabbath comes to us weekly, bringing larger opportunities for rest, meditation, and communion with the Creator. Before its blessed and precious effects have been lost, the approach of another Sabbath renews its hallowing influence. Thus it sweetens all days and extends its blessing to all our time, as we *"remember* the sabbath day, to keep it holy."

The New Testament Sabbath

The New Testament does not change in the smallest degree the obligation to observe the seventh day commanded by God. Christ observed this day during the entire period of His earthly life. The disciples observed this day uniformly during the period of their lives, while establishing the first Christian churches. There is no occasion on record in the New Testament where any human being endeavored to keep the first day as a sabbath.

The Sabbath of the New Testament is the Sabbath of the Old Testament, the seventh day of the week.

Divine Authority for the Change Lacking

JESUS CHRIST did not change the Sabbath. As Creator He had brought it into existence. He designed it to be a memorial of His power in the work of both Creation and redemption. When He came into the world to carry out the eternal purpose of human salvation, it is scarcely conceivable that He would set aside the memorial which He Himself had established to commemorate His finished work of redemption.

Neither the disciples of Christ nor the early Christian churches ever heard of such a thing as a divine change in Sabbath observance. Hence the observance of any other day than the seventh as the Sabbath is unknown in the New Testament. Sunday observance by Christian believers is of later origin than the times of the Bible.

Indeed, no insignificant part of the public teaching and work of Christ will be found to have been given to setting forth what it is lawful and right to do on the seventh day, which is rather difficult of explanation by those who profess to believe He abolished the Sabbath.

The observance of the Sabbath by the Jewish people in the time of Christ had come to be entirely unlike that which God designed it to be. So far from being a blessing, it had come to be a burden.

Satan had done his best by seductive temptations to cause the Jews to relinquish the observance of the Sabbath. In this he was partially successful. God permitted His people to go into the Babylonian captivity because of their sins, which included Sabbathbreaking. Upon their return from the Captivity the Jews resolved to keep the Sabbath with the utmost faithfulness, as God had commanded. But again the evil one determined to ensnare them, and succeeded in leading them to pervert both the meaning and the purpose of the Sabbath, until it was loaded with burdensome restrictions.

When Jesus appeared as a public teacher among the Jews, He missed no opportunity to correct the false conceptions of the Sabbath. He seized upon every occasion to free the day from its burdensome, man-made regulations.

Miracles on the Sabbath

Indeed, He made such occasions, for He purposely selected the Sabbath as the day on which to do many of His miracles and works of mercy.

In Capernaum, in the synagogue and on the Sabbath day, He cast the "spirit of an unclean devil" out of the man whom it had bound. Later, on the same Sabbath, He healed "Simon's wife's mother" of "a great fever." (See Luke 4:30-39.)

Such acts performed on the Sabbath were looked upon with serious question by the Jews, for they would not bring Him their sick upon the Sabbath, but waited until "even, when the sun did set." (See Mark 1:32-34; Luke 4:40.)

Jesus, however, continued to correct their views regarding what constituted real Sabbathkeeping, and to bring about a reform in the observance of the Sabbath. In order to convince them that He spoke with authority in the matter, He took occasion, in connection with the incident of His disciples' plucking the ears of corn on the Sabbath, to declare that "the Son of man is Lord even of the sabbath day." (See Matthew 12:1-8.) In this same connection He gave helpful instruction regarding the nature of true Sabbathkeeping.

Christ Risked His Life to Free the Sabbath

So necessary was it to free the Sabbath from the wicked traditions surrounding it, which went so far as to prevent the doing of anything on that day toward the healing of the sick, that Christ braved the malice of the Pharisees and risked His life in order to free the Sabbath from these perverted restrictions. When He healed the man with the withered hand in the synagogue upon the Sabbath, and in connection therewith gave much-needed instruction as to the proper observance of the day, the Pharisees, in anger, "held a council against him, how they might destroy him." (See Matthew 12:9-14.)

He healed the impotent man at the pool of Bethesda, healed him of an infirmity of thirty-eight years' standing. When this was complained of, and the Jews persecuted Jesus and "sought to slay him," He once more seized the occasion to give them sound instruction regarding Sabbath observance, saying, "My Father worketh hitherto, and I work." (See John 5:1-19.)

Months later this same case of healing was brought under discussion, and He again enlightened His enemies regarding the meaning of the Sabbath. (See John 7:21-23.)

Rescuing the Sabbath From Burdensome Restrictions

The Jews refused, however, to receive instruction, and the Lord found it necessary to continue His work in behalf of the Sabbath, the work of rescuing it from the perversions that

PAUL REMMEY, ARTIST

Christ cleared the Sabbath of the burdensome restrictions placed on it by the Jews. He healed the sick on the sacred day, bringing relief to the suffering.

concealed from the multitude its true purpose and prevented many from finding in it spiritual blessing and rest.

On the Sabbath He met a man who was born blind, and in compassion moistened clay, anointed the blind eyes, and sent the man to a pool to wash. The man went, washed, and received his sight. This making of the clay and healing of the blind was looked upon as a violation of the Sabbath by His bigoted enemies, whereas it was the perfection of Sabbath-keeping. (See John 9:1-38.)

Later, on another Sabbath, He healed a woman who had been bound by Satan eighteen years, and could not stand erect. He met the clamor of His opponents by giving further instruction regarding genuine Sabbathkeeping, silencing them and bringing gladness to the people. (See Luke 13:10-17.)

He gave additional instruction on the proper observance of the Sabbath at a Sabbath dinner in a Pharisee's house, during which He healed the man afflicted with dropsy. (See Luke 14:1-6.)

So the history of the ministry of Christ reveals Him as a true Sabbathkeeper. He put forth sustained effort to correct long-established errors regarding the Sabbath, endeavoring to free it of the rigors and burdens of Pharisaic tradition.

Certainly, in the face of such a record, it is folly to maintain that the Lord of the Sabbath intended to do away with the observance of the seventh day. Had such been His purpose He would not have devoted so much of His public ministry to the work of instructing the people how rightly to keep this day.

It is most unfair, to put it mildly, for Christian teachers today, in order to carry out their purpose of turning the minds of men against the Sabbath of the Bible, to represent these man-made restrictions and Pharisaic rigors as really belonging to the Sabbath of God, and thus construe Christ's long-continued and powerful effort to rid the Sabbath of these perversions as a proof of His violation of God's Sabbath commandment and as an effort to discredit the Sabbath itself. Those who do this, in reality take their stand against the Lord of the Sabbath, and join the ancient Pharisees in saying, "This man is not of God, because he keepeth not the sabbath day" (John 9:16).

First Day Mentioned Six Times in the Gospels

The four Gospels mention the first day of the week six times, and in these texts those who observe the first day must find their warrant for such observance. The passages in the Gospels which refer to the first day are Matthew 28:1; Mark 16:1, 2, 9; Luke 23:56 and 24:1; John 20:1, 19.

Here, if anywhere, must be sought whatever authority there is for Sunday sacredness. These texts speak of "the first day of the week." They unite in declaring that the resurrection of our Lord took place on that day. Sunday observers claim that the occurrence of this event on that day brought about a change of the Sabbath from the seventh day to the first. If this is so, these passages should make it clear.

But an examination of these passages reveals that they say nothing whatever about a change of the Sabbath. They speak of the Sabbath, it is true, but they most carefully discriminate between the Sabbath and the first day of the week, making it plain that the Sabbath of the New Testament is the day before the first day. They give no sacred title to the first day. They *do* give such a title to the seventh day. They do not say that Christ rested on the first day, which would have been essential to its becoming a Sabbath. They say nothing about any blessing being placed upon the first day. They do not tell us that Christ ever said anything about the first day, either as a holy day or otherwise. They give no precept or command regarding its observance. There is nothing in these passages declaring that the first day is to be looked upon by the followers of Christ as anything more than the ordinary weekday that it is called——just "the first day of the week."

No Authority for Sunday Sacredness

After giving full consideration to all these passages, Smith's Dictionary of the Bible, in its article on "The Lord's Day," makes this admission:

"Taken separately, perhaps, and even all together, these passages seem scarcely adequate to prove that the dedication of the first day of the week to the purposes above mentioned was a matter of apostolic institution, or even of apostolic practice."——Page 356.

Hence there is no evidence in these passages to cause any follower of our Lord to believe that they contain any authority at all for Sunday sacredness.

Instead of its being true that Jesus blessed and hallowed the first day, the fact is that He never once mentioned the first day. He did not even take its name upon His lips, so far as we have any record.

First Day Mentioned Once in the Acts

The first day of the week is mentioned in but two other places in the New Testament. The first of these is in the book of Acts: "Upon the first day of the week, when the disciples came together to break bread, Paul preached unto them, ready to depart on the morrow; and continued his speech until midnight. And there were many lights in the upper chamber, where they were gathered together" (Acts 20:7, 8).

Here is the record of a religious meeting that was held on the first day of the week. In passing, it should be noticed that this is the only instance recorded in the New Testament where a religious meeting was held on the first day.

This passage, however, contains no evidence of a change of the Sabbath, and no support for Sunday sacredness. It was a first-day meeting, but not a Sunday meeting. It was held at night. "There were many lights," and Paul "continued his speech until midnight." The only night there is to the Bible first day is what we now know as Saturday night. Bible days begin and end at sunset. The Bible first day begins at sunset Saturday night and is over at sunset Sunday night. The "midnight," therefore, to which Paul "continued his speech" must have been, could only have been, Saturday night.

Conybeare and Howson, in their deservedly popular *Life and Epistles of the Apostle Paul,* dealing with the time when this meeting was held, make these remarks:

"It was the evening which succeeded the Jewish Sabbath. On the Sunday morning the vessel was about to sail."— Scribner's ed., Vol. II, p. 206.

Dr. Horatio B. Hackett, professor of New Testament Greek in Rochester Theological Seminary, in his *Commentary on Acts,* says:

"The Jews reckoned the day from evening to morning, and on that principle the evening of the first day of the week would be our Saturday evening. If Luke reckoned so here, as many commentators suppose, the apostle then waited for the expiration of the Jewish Sabbath, and held his last religious service with the brethren at Troas . . . on Saturday evening, and consequently resumed his journey on Sunday morning."— Edition of 1882, pages 221, 222.

The account in Acts telling of this night meeting was written by Luke thirty years, at least, after the crucifixion of Christ. It is significant that in referring to the first day he does not call it by a sacred title or name. He says nothing about its supposedly sacred character. He speaks of it merely as one of the weekdays, "the first" of the seven.

There is no support for Sunday sacredness in this passsage.

The Final Mention of the First Day

The final mention of the first day of the week in the Bible is in the writings of Paul, the only time the writer of these Epistles, or any of the Epistles of the New Testament, refers to the day in any connection: "Now concerning the collection for the saints, as I have given order to the churches of Galatia, even so do ye. Upon the first day of the week let every one of you lay by him in store, as God hath prospered him, that there be no gatherings when I come" (1 Corinthians 16: 1, 2).

It is argued from this passage that the first day must have been the day for public worship in the churches of Corinth and Galatia, and if in these, then most probably in the other apostolic churches as well, and that therefore the Sabbath had been changed to that day. This, however, is getting out of the text far more than it even remotely implies.

No Sunday Meeting

This passage arranges for precisely the *reverse* of a public collection. Each believer in Corinth was to *lay by himself in store* as God had prospered him, not take his offering to a place of meeting, not hold any meeting at all on that day for public worship. The Greek lexicon of Greenfield translates the Greek here, "with one's self, i.e., at home."

Sir William Domville, in his book *The Sabbath,* has these

comments on the claims that are sometimes made regarding the significance of this passage:

"Strange that a text which says nothing of any meeting for any purpose, should be brought to prove a custom to meet for purposes of religion! . . .

"If it be strange to infer from it a custom to meet, although no meeting is mentioned in it, it seems still more strange, still more inconsistent, to infer from it . . . that a direction to lay by alms at home means that those alms should be given at church. . . .

"The translation in our common Bibles is just to the original: 'Let every one of you lay by him in store.' A still more literal translation of the word in the original, *thēsaurizōn* [treasuring up], would render it still more apparent that each contributor was to make the accumulation himself, and not to hand it over from week to week to any other person."—Pages 101-104.

There is nothing in this passage to show that the early churches were observing Sunday as the Sabbath. The first day is mentioned, indeed, but merely as one of the days of the week, the day on which, after they had observed the Sabbath and had returned to their weekly toil and started a new week of business, they were to cast up accounts, determine the gains of the preceding week, and, learning how God had prospered them, lay aside a proportion of their gains for the famine-stricken brethren elsewhere.

Ceremonial Sabbaths Discontinued

It is supposed by some that Paul had reference to the change of the Sabbath when he wrote to the Colossians: "Let no man therefore judge you in . . . respect of an holyday, or of the new moon, or of the sabbath days: which are a shadow of things to come; but the body is of Christ" (Colossians 2:16, 17).

The ceremonial system of the Old Testament had many festivals, holy days, annual sabbaths. That system, "imposed on them until the time of reformation" (Hebrews 9:10), had passed away with Christ, whom it had foreshadowed. The believer in Christ was not, therefore, to return to its types and shadows. He did not need to observe its seven annual sabbaths (Leviticus 23:4, 24, 32, 39), all of which were to be kept in addition to or "beside the sabbaths of the Lord" (Leviticus 23:38). And as these ceremonial and ritual observances were no longer binding, the Christian believer is, in this passage in Colossians, exhorted not to permit any man to judge him in these things. This passage has no reference at all to the seventh-day Sabbath of the Lord.

Perhaps this will be received more readily, and be seen more clearly, if attention is called to the comment on this passage by noted authorities. Dr. Adam Clarke, in the commentary that bears his name, says concerning Colossians 2:16:

"There is no intimation here that the *Sabbath* was done away, or that its moral use was superseded by the introduction of Christianity. I have shown elsewhere that, *Remember the Sabbath day, to keep it holy,* is a command of *perpetual obligation,* and can never be superseded but by the final termination of time. As it is a *type* of that rest which remains for the people of God, of an eternity of bliss, it must continue in full force till that eternity arrives; for no *type* ever ceases till the *antitype* be come. Besides, it is not clear that the apostle refers at all to the *Sabbath* in this place, whether Jewish or Christian; his *sabbaton, of Sabbaths* or *weeks,* most probably refers to their *feasts of weeks,* of which much has been said in the notes on the Pentateuch."—Edition of 1851.

Dr. Albert Barnes, the well-known Presbyterian commentator, in his *Notes on Colossians* (2:16), writes thus:

" 'Or of the sabbath days.' The word 'sabbath' in the Old Testament is applied not only to the seventh day, but to all the days of holy rest that were observed by the Hebrews, and particularly to the beginning and close of their great festivals. There is, doubtless, reference to those days in this place, as the word is used in the plural number, and the apostle does not refer particularly to *the* Sabbath properly so called. There is no evidence from this passage that he would teach that there was no obligation to observe *any* holy time, for there is not the slightest reason to believe that he meant to teach that one of the ten commandments had ceased to be binding on mankind.

"If he had used the word in the singular number, '*the* Sabbath,' it would then, of course, have been clear that he meant to teach that that commandment had ceased to be binding, and that a Sabbath was no longer to be observed. But the use of the term in the plural number, and the connection, show that he had his eye on the great number of days which were observed by the Hebrews as festivals, as a part of their ceremonial and typical law, and not to the moral law, or the ten commandments. No part of the moral law—no one of the ten commandments—could be spoken of as '*a shadow* of good things to come.' These commandments are, from the nature of .moral law, of perpetual and universal obligation."— Edition of 1850, pp. 306, 307.

We conclude, therefore, after careful examination of the New Testament, that it contains no evidence of a change of the Sabbath, no divine authority for such a change, and no support in even the smallest degree for Sunday observance.

How, Why, and by Whom the Change Was Brought About

THE change from the true Sabbath to the false sabbath was brought about by the great apostasy in the early church, which crystallized into the Roman Catholic system. The reasons that prompted this apostate movement to discard the Sabbath of the Lord and adopt the day of the sun worshipers were principally twofold: namely, a desire to avoid being identified with the Jews, whose bigotry and downfall had made them unpopular; and an equally strong desire to win the pagan sun worshipers and gain their adherence to the church.

Even in the days of the apostles the great apostasy had begun to develop. Paul wrote: "The mystery of iniquity doth already work" (2 Thessalonians 2:7).

He declared again: "I know this, that after my departing shall grievous wolves enter in among you, not sparing the flock. Also of your own selves shall men arise, speaking perverse things, to draw away disciples after them" (Acts 20:29, 30).

Antichrist the Author of Sunday Observance

This departure from the faith would widen and grow to great proportions, said the apostle. A great "falling away," or apostasy, would ultimately disclose "that man of sin," "the

31

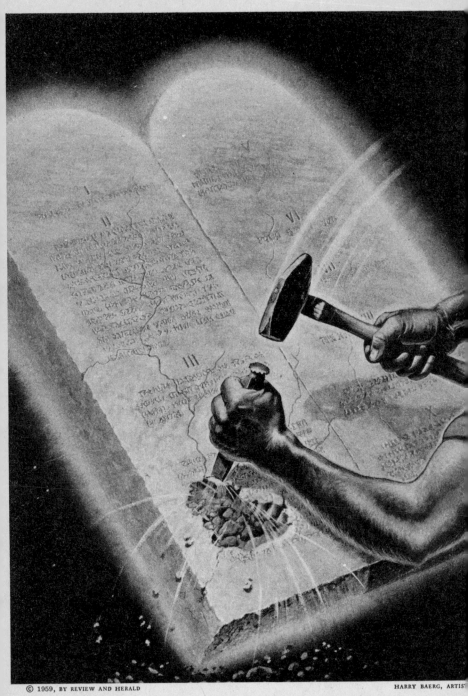

HARRY BAERG, ARTIST

Unholy hands have, in effect, chiseled the Sabbath command from the law by substituting another day for the one set apart by God.

son of perdition; who opposeth and exalteth himself above all that is called God, or that is worshipped; so that he as God sitteth in the temple of God, shewing himself that he is God" (2 Thessalonians 2:3, 4).

"This," according to the apostle John, "is that spirit of antichrist, whereof ye have heard that it should come; and even now already is it in the world" (1 John 4:3).

Fulfilling these predictions, Christian faith and Christian polity changed their entire aspect between the days of the apostles and the professed conversion of Constantine, the emperor of Rome. Truth was changed into error, and perversions of the true faith multiplied with astonishing rapidity.

"Rites and ceremonies, of which neither Paul nor Peter ever heard, crept silently into use, and then claimed the rank of divine institutions. Officers for whom the primitive disciples could have found no place, and titles which to them would have been altogether unintelligible, began to challenge attention, and to be named apostolic."—WILLIAM D. KILLEN, D.D., *The Ancient Church,* Preface to original edition, p. xvi.

Among these strange, new, and false observances that were brought into the practice of the fallen church, was the festival of Sunday.

Regarding this apostasy, and the origin of Sunday observance among Christians resulting from it, together with the reasons back of the adoption of this pagan festival day, a great mass of historical testimony can be introduced. That which is here submitted is taken from the writings of those only who have been or are observers of Sunday, for their admissions regarding the origin of this observance will be of greater weight than charges that might be made by Sabbathkeepers.

Wilhelm August Johann Neander, the great German theologian and historian of Heidelberg, whose *History of the Christian Religion and Church* is of such value and merit as to have gained for him the title "prince of church historians," frankly declares:

"Opposition to Judaism introduced the particular festival of Sunday very early, indeed, into the place of the Sabbath. . . . The festival of Sunday, like all other festivals, was always only a human ordinance, and it was far from the intentions of the apostles to establish a divine command in this respect, far from them, and from the early apostolic church, to transfer the laws of the Sabbath to Sunday. Perhaps, at the end of the second century a false application of this kind had begun to take place; for men appear by that time to have considered laboring on Sunday as a sin."—Rose's translation from the first German edition, p. 186.

Sabbath Observance Not Discontinued

The observance of the seventh day was not discontinued by the early Christians for a considerable time after Christ's ascension. Hundreds of years had elapsed before the might and power of the Papacy were able to drive it out of the church. As a matter of fact, it has never been entirely discontinued, as there has always been a righteous seed who have remained true and loyal to God's holy Sabbath.

Mr. Morer, a learned clergyman of the Church of England, says that "the primitive Christians had a great veneration for the Sabbath, and spent the day in devotion and sermons. And it is not to be doubted but they derived this practice from the apostles themselves."—*Dialogues on the Lord's Day,* p. 189.

Says Prof. Edward Brerewood, of Gresham College, London, of the same church:

"The ancient Sabbath did remain and was observed . . . by the Christians of the East Church, above three hundred years after our Saviour's death."—*A Learned Treatise of the Sabbath*, p. 77.

The careful and candid theologian and historian, Lyman Coleman, says:

"Down even to the fifth century the observance of the Jewish Sabbath was continued in the Christian church, but with a rigor and solemnity gradually diminishing until it was wholly discontinued."—*Ancient Christianity Exemplified*, chap. 26, sec. 2, p. 527.

Socrates, a Greek church historian of the fifth century, whose work was a continuation of that of Eusebius, says:

"Almost all churches throughout the world celebrate the sacred mysteries on the Sabbath of every week, yet the Christians of Alexandria and at Rome, on account of some ancient tradition, have ceased to do this."—*Ecclesiastical History* v. 22. 21, 22, in *A Select Library of Nicene and Post-Nicene Fathers*, 2d series, Vol. II, p. 132.

Sozomen, another church historian of the fifth century, asserts:

"The people of Constantinople, and almost everywhere, assemble together on the Sabbath, as well as on the first day of the week, which custom is never observed at Rome or at Alexandria."—*Ecclesiastical History*, vii. 19, in *A Select Library of Nicene and Post-Nicene Fathers*, 2d series, Vol. II, p. 390.

A Pagan Institution Grafted Upon Christianity

On this point that Sunday was not known as a rest day in the early centuries, these statements occur in Smith and Cheetham's Dictionary of Christian Antiquities:

"The notion of a formal substitution by apostolic authority of the Lord's day for the Jewish Sabbath, and the transference to it, perhaps in a spiritualized form, of the Sabbatical obligation established by the promulgation of the fourth commandment, has no basis whatever, either in Holy Scripture or in Christian antiquity. . . . The idea afterwards embodied in the title of the 'Christian Sabbath,' and carried out in ordinances of Judaic rigor, was, so far as we can see, entirely unknown in the early centuries of Christianity."—Article "Sabbath," p. 1823.

Hutton Webster, Ph.D., in his *Rest Days,* has this to say:

"The early Christians had at first adopted the Jewish seven-day week with its numbered week days, but by the close of the third century A.D. this began to give way to the planetary week; and in the fourth and fifth centuries the pagan designations became generally accepted in the western half of Christendom. The use of the planetary names by Christians attests the growing influence of astrological speculations introduced by converts from paganism. . . . During these same centuries the spread of Oriental solar worships, especially that of Mithra [Persian sun worship], in the Roman world, had already led to the substitution by pagans of *dies Solis* for *dies Saturni,* as the first day of the planetary week. . . . Thus gradually a pagan institution was engrafted on Christianity."—Pages 220, 221.

Corruptions of Christianity

Sunday observance began at an early period in the history of the church. Its early introduction is not, however, an argument for its genuineness as a Scriptural obligation. Only a Scriptural command is sufficient for that. And there is no such Scriptural command for Sunday observance.

There is no Bible authority for the introduction of any of the corruptions that were brought into the early church, and which later developed into the Papacy. On this, Dowling, in his *History of Romanism,* remarks:

"There is scarcely anything which strikes the mind of the careful student of ancient ecclesiastical history with greater surprise than the comparatively early period at which many of the corruptions of Christianity, which are embodied in the Romish system, took their rise; yet it is not to be supposed that when the first originators of many of these unscriptural notions and practices planted those germs of corruption, they anticipated or even imagined they would ever grow into such a vast and hideous system of superstition and error as is that of popery."—Thirteenth ed., i. 1, sec. 1, p. 65.

The Day of the Sun Borrowed From Heathenism

The motives that prompted the change from the true Sabbath to the day of the sun are further described by a Church of England rector, the Reverend T. H. Morer, in his book *Six Dialogues on the Lord's Day:*

"It is not to be denied but we borrow the name of this day from the ancient Greeks and Romans, and we allow that the old Egyptians worshiped the sun, and as a standing *memorial* of their veneration, dedicated this day to him. And we find by the influence of their examples, *other* nations, and among them the Jews themselves, doing him homage; yet these abuses did not hinder the Fathers of the Christian church simply to repeal, or altogether lay by, the day or its name, but only to sanctify and improve both, as they did also the pagan temples polluted before with idolatrous services, and other instances wherein those good men were always tender to work any other change than what was evidently necessary, and in such things as were plainly inconsistent with the Christian religion; so that Sunday being the day on which the Gentiles solemnly adored that planet, and called it Sunday, partly from its influence on that day especially, and partly in respect to its divine body (as they conceived it), the Christians thought fit to keep the same day and the same name of it, that they might not appear causelessly peevish, and by that means hinder the conversion of the Gentiles, and bring a greater prejudice than might be otherwise taken against the gospel."—Pages 22, 23.

Amalgamation of Corrupt Christianity and Paganism

It thus appears that the amalgamation between corrupt Christianity and paganism that produced Roman Catholicism was the soil in which also grew the observance of the counterfeit sabbath, namely, Sunday. The Catholic system and Sunday belong together. Both originated in paganism, and both were grafted upon the Christian church at the same time. They both swept the field of all opposition, and became ruling factors in Christendom. After they became established, they both sought to trace their origin back to apostolic times. The pope claimed to be the successor of Peter, and Sunday claimed for its origin the day of Christ's resurrection. Neither claim was true, nor has either claim been established. Nevertheless both of these frauds grew to enormous size and power, the pope becoming lord of bishops and Sunday the lord of days; but their success drove the Lord of life out of the church, and left only antichrist.

One of the apologists for this pagan day in those early years, Tertullian, recognized as an ecclesiastical writer by the Catholic Church, addressed a book to the nations still in idolatry, and in it endeavored to meet the confusion created by the adoption of Sunday by Christians, which had given rise to the thought that they were going over to sun worship altogether. He says:

"Others, with greater regard to good manners, it must be confessed, suppose that the sun is the God of the Christians, because it is a well-known fact that we pray toward the east, or because we make Sunday a day of festivity. What then? Do you do less than this? Do not many among you, with an affectation of sometimes worshiping the heavenly bodies likewise move your lips in the direction of the sunrise? It is you, at all events, who have even admitted the sun into the calendar of the week; and you have selected its day [Sunday] in preference to the preceding day, as the most suitable in the week for either an entire abstinence from the bath, or for its postponement until the evening, or for taking rest and for banqueting. By resorting to these customs, you deliberately deviate from your own religious rites to those of strangers."—*Ad Nationes,* i. 13, in *The Ante-Nicene Fathers,* Vol. III, p. 123.

The only defense that this early Christian writer could make for adopting Sunday from the heathen was to ask the question, "Do you do less than this?" It was the pagans, he points out, who had "admitted the sun into the calendar of the week," and who had preferred Sunday above "the preceding day," which was the Sabbath. How, then, he argues, could they chide the Christians for following their own example? This is certainly evidence enough regarding the source from which Sunday observance originated.

The Earliest Sunday Law Known to History

The earliest Sunday law known to history is that of Constantine, promulgated in A.D. 321. It reads:

"On the venerable day of the sun let the magistrates and

The earliest law known to history that called people to worship on the first day of the week was promulgated by the Roman emperor Constantine in A.D. 321.

people residing in cities rest, and let all workshops be closed. In the country, however, persons engaged in agriculture may freely and lawfully continue their pursuits; because it often happens that another day is not so suitable for grain sowing or for vine planting; lest by neglecting the proper moment for such operations the bounty of heaven should be lost. (Given the 7th day of March, Crispus and Constantine being consuls each of them for the second time.)—*Codex Justinianus,* lib. 3, tit. 12, 3; translated in PHILIP SCHAFF, D.D., *History of the Christian Church* (seven-volume edition, 1902), Vol. III, p. 380.

Constantine was emperor of Rome from A.D. 306 to 337. He was a sun worshiper during the first years of his reign. Later he professed conversion to Christianity, but at heart remained a devotee of the sun.

Of his religion, Edward Gibbon, in his *Decline and Fall of the Roman Empire,* says:

"The devotion of Constantine was more peculiarly directed to the genius of the sun, the Apollo of Greek and Roman mythology; and he was pleased to be represented with the symbols of the god of light and poetry. The unerring shafts of that deity, the brightness of his eyes, his laurel wreath, immortal beauty, and elegant accomplishments, seem to point him out as the patron of a young hero. The altars of Apollo were crowned with the votive offerings of Constantine; and the credulous multitude were taught to believe that the emperor was permitted to behold with mortal eyes the visible majesty of their tutelar deity; and that, either waking or in a vision, he was blessed with the auspicious omens of a long and victorious reign. The sun was universally celebrated as the invincible guide and protector of Constantine."—Chapter 20, par. 3.

Sunday and Sun Worship

The legislation inaugurated by Constantine for the establishment of Sunday observance is thus referred to by two encyclopedias:

"The earliest recognition of the observance of Sunday as a legal duty is a constitution of Constantine in 321 A.D., enacting that all courts of justice, inhabitants of towns, and workshops were to be at rest on Sunday (*venerabili die solis*), with an exception in favor of those engaged in agricultural labor."
—*Encyclopaedia Britannica* (11th ed.), art. "Sunday."

"Unquestionably the first law, either ecclesiastical or civil, by which the Sabbatical observance of that day is known to have been ordained, is the edict of Constantine, 321 A.D."—*Chambers' Encyclopaedia* (1882 ed.), Vol. VIII, p. 401, art. "Sabbath."

That this Sunday legislation had no connection with Christianity is clearly seen when the facts contained in the following quotation are considered:

"This legislation by Constantine probably bore no relation to Christianity; it appears, on the contrary, that the emperor, in his capacity as Pontifex Maximus, was only adding the day of the sun, the worship of which was then firmly established in the Roman Empire, to the other ferial days of the sacred calendar."—HUTTON WEBSTER, Ph.D., *Rest Days*, pp. 122, 123.

Strengthening Sunday Observance by Law

Following this initial legislation, both emperors and popes in succeeding centuries added other laws to strengthen Sunday observance.

"What began, however, as a pagan ordinance, ended as a Christian regulation; and a long series of imperial decrees, during the fourth, fifth, and sixth centuries, enjoined with increasing stringency abstinence from labor on Sunday."—*Ibid.*, p. 270.

What these further steps were which both church and state took to make certain that Sunday should displace the Sabbath, are covered in a few paragraphs by a distinguished lawyer of Baltimore, Maryland, James T. Ringgold:

"In 386, under Gratian, Valentinian, and Theodosius, it was decreed that all litigation and business should cease [on Sunday]. . . .

"Among the doctrines laid down in a letter of Pope Innocent I, written in the last year of his papacy (416), is that Saturday should be observed as a fast day. . . .

"In 425, under Theodosius the Younger, abstinence from theatricals and the circus [on Sunday] was enjoined. . . .

"In 538, at a council at Orleans, . . . it was ordained that everything previously permitted on Sunday should still be lawful; but that work at the plow, or in the vineyard, and cutting, reaping, threshing, tilling, and hedging should be abstained from, that people might more conveniently attend church. . . .

"About 590 Pope Gregory, in a letter to the Roman people, denounced as the prophets of Antichrist those who maintained that work ought not to be done on the seventh day."—*The Law of Sunday*, pp. 265-267.

The closing paragraph of the foregoing quotation indicates that there were still those in the church at late as A.D. 590 who were both observing and teaching the observance of the Bible Sabbath. Indeed, such observance on the part of a faithful few has been followed throughout all the Christian centuries. Among those classed as Waldenses there were observers of the seventh day.

Neander asks:

"May we not suppose that from very ancient times a party of Judaizing Christians had survived, of which this sect [the Pasaginians, classed among the Waldenses by some authorities] must be regarded as an offshoot?"—*Church History, Fifth Period,* section 4, 15th American ed., Vol. IV, p. 591.

The ecclesiastical and civil laws just referred to in the development of Sunday legislation make clear that Eusebius, a noted bishop of the Catholic Church, the reputed father of ecclesiastical history, and a flatterer and biographer of Constantine, was justified in saying:

"All things whatsoever that it was duty to do on the Sabbath, these we have transferred to the Lord's day."—*Commentary on the Psalms, Comment on Psalms 91 (92 in Authorized Version),* quoted in ROBERT COX, *Literature of the Sabbath Question,* Vol. I, p. 361.

Substituting a Pagan Day for God's Day

This substitution of Sunday for the Sabbath is not a thing which the Catholic Church either denies or attempts to conceal. On the contrary, it frankly admits it, and indeed points to it with pride as evidence of its power to change even a commandment of God. Read these extracts from Catholic catechisms:

The Convert's Catechism of Catholic Doctrine, the work of the Reverend Peter Geiermann, C.S.R., received on January 25, 1910, the "apostolic blessing" of Pope Pius X. On this subject of the change of the Sabbath, this catechism says:

"*Ques.*—Which is the Sabbath day?

"*Ans.*—Saturday is the Sabbath day.

"*Ques.*—Why do we observe Sunday instead of Saturday?

"*Ans.*—We observe Sunday instead of Saturday because the Catholic Church, in the Council of Laodicea (A.D. 336), transferred the solemnity from Saturday to Sunday."—Second edition, p. 50.

A Doctrinal Catechism, by the Reverend Stephen Keenan, was approved by the Most Reverend John Hughes, D.D., Archbishop of New York. It has these remarks on the question of the change of the Sabbath:

"*Ques.*—Have you any other way of proving that the church has power to institute festivals of precept?

"*Ans.*—Had she not such power, she could not have done that in which all modern religionists agree with her— she could not have substituted the observance of Sunday the first day of the week, for the observance of Saturday the "seventh day, a change for which there is no Scriptural authority." —Page 174.

An Abridgment of the Christian Doctrine, by the Reverend Henry Tuberville, D.D., of Douay College, France, contains these questions and answers:

"*Ques.*—How prove you that the church hath power to command feasts and holy days?

"*Ans.*—By the very act of changing the Sabbath into Sunday, which Protestants allow of; and therefore they fondly contradict themselves, by keeping Sunday strictly, and breaking most other feasts commanded by the same church.

"*Ques.*—How prove you that?

"*Ans.*—Because by keeping Sunday, they acknowledge the church's power to ordain feasts, and to command them under sin; and by not keeping the rest [of the feast days] by her commanded, they again deny, in fact, the same power."— Page 58.

Not a Single Bible Line for Sunday Observance

Cardinal Gibbons, in *The Faith of Our Fathers,* says this:

"You may read the Bible from Genesis to Revelation, and you will not find a single line authorizing the sanctification of Sunday. The Scriptures enforce the religious observance of Saturday, a day which we never sanctify."—Edition of 1893, p. 111.

"The Catholic Church . . . Changed the Day"

The *Catholic Press* of Sydney, Australia, is emphatic that Sunday observance is solely of Catholic origin.

"Sunday is a Catholic institution, and its claims to observance can be defended only on Catholic principles. . . . From beginning to end of Scripture there is not a single passage that warrants the transfer of weekly public worship from the last day of the week to the first."—August 25, 1900.

In his book *Plain Talk About the Protestantism of Today,* Monsignor Segur says:

"It was the Catholic Church which, by the authority of Jesus Christ, has transferred this rest to the Sunday in remembrance of the resurrection of our Lord. Thus the observance of Sunday by the Protestants is an homage they pay, in spite of themselves, to the authority of the [Catholic] Church."— Edition of 1868, Part 3, sec. 14, p. 225.

In the year 1893 the *Catholic Mirror,* of Baltimore, Maryland, was the official organ of Cardinal Gibbons. In its issue of September 23 of that year it published this striking statement:

"The Catholic Church for over one thousand years before the existence of a Protestant, by virtue of her divine mission, changed the day from Saturday to Sunday." "The Christian Sabbath is therefore to this day the acknowledged offspring of the Catholic Church as spouse of the Holy Ghost, without a word of remonstrance from the Protestant world."—Reprinted by the *Catholic Mirror* as a pamphlet, *The Christian Sabbath,* pp. 29, 31.

Sunday Observance Without Divine Authority

Burns and Oates, of London, are publishers of Roman Catholic books, one of which they are pleased to call *The Library of Christian Doctrine.* A part of this is called "Why Don't You Keep the Sabbath Day?" and sets forth the following argument of a Catholic with a Protestant:

"You will tell me that Saturday was the Jewish Sabbath, but that the Christian Sabbath has been changed to Sunday. Changed! but by whom? Who has the authority to change an express commandment of Almighty God? When God has spoken and said, 'Thou shalt keep holy the seventh day,' who shall dare to say, Nay, thou mayest work and do all manner of worldly business on the seventh day; but thou shalt keep holy the first day in its stead? This is a most important question, which I know not how you can answer.

"You are a Protestant, and you profess to go by the Bible and the Bible only; and yet in so important a matter as the observance of one day in seven as a holy day, you go against the plain letter of the Bible, and put another day in the place of that day which the Bible has commanded. The command to keep holy the seventh day is one of the ten commandments; you believe that the other nine are still binding; who gave you authority to tamper with the fourth? If you are consistent with your own principles, if you really follow the Bible and the Bible only, you ought to be able to produce some portion of the New Testament in which this fourth commandment is expressly altered."—Pages 3, 4.

After a careful examination of the Bible, of history, both

civil and ecclesiastical, of theological writings, commentaries, church manuals, catechisms, and the candid admissions of Sunday observers, we are compelled to conclude that there is no authority in the Holy Scriptures for the observance of Sunday, no authority given to man to make such a change from the seventh to the first day, no divine sanction given the change now that man has made it; that this substitution of a false sabbath for the true Sabbath of the Lord was entirely the work of an anti-Christian movement which adopted the observance of a purely pagan day and presumptuously established it in the Christian church; and that this observance has no binding obligation upon Christian believers, but should be instantly discarded as a matter of practice, and the true Sabbath of God restored to its rightful place, both in the hearts of His people and in the practice of His church.

The Identical Seventh Day

DIFFER as men may regarding the identity of the Sabbath today, there can be no difference of opinion regarding this fact: The seventh day of the creative week was set apart from the other days, a distinction being made between it and the other days, and it was declared to be the blessed, holy rest day of the Creator. This is the record: "Thus the heavens and the earth were finished, and all the host of them. And on the seventh day God ended his work which he had made; and he rested on the seventh day from all his work which he had made. And God blessed the seventh day, and sanctified it: because that in it he had rested from all his work which God created and made" (Genesis 2:1-3).

If the seventh day has been lost since that time, it was not lost then. It was the last day of the week, the seventh.

The claim is now made that this identical seventh day of Creation cannot be located. We are informed that to attempt to identify it now would prove a hopeless task, altogether impossible. The reason for this is said to be the confusion that has come in as a result of many changes in calendars between that time and this, the entire absence of any calendar at all in primitive times, and the failure to keep any accurate account of the times the earth has rotated on its axis through the centuries.

HARRY ANDERSON, ARTIST

The first seventh day of time was occupied by Adam and Eve in holy rest and worship, for "God blessed the seventh day, and sanctified it."

These are the reasons, so we are told, that make the task of finding the seventh day at this late period in the world's history an altogether insurmountable one.

If men really desire, however, to find the seventh day, it can be done. It is not such a task as it is presumed to be. If there is a genuine desire to know the truth there is always a way to discover it.

God Keeps Accurate Record

God did not leave this matter of an accurate keeping of records entirely in the hands of men. Their methods of reckoning the passing of time, their counting of the days, their calendars and almanacs, need not be taken as our sole reliance in identifying the seventh day. God has a way of taking care of His own institutions and ordinances, as well as His own people, upon which we are safe to place full reliance.

There surely can be no question that God attached very great importance to the observance of the seventh-day Sabbath. He descended from heaven on Mount Sinai, and in the hearing of perhaps three million people spoke the words of the Ten Commandment law. Among the audible words from His lips were these: "The seventh day is the sabbath of the Lord thy God: in it thou shalt not do any work" (Exodus 20:10).

God attached a very definite and solemn penalty to the violation of this law. He has declared the transgression of the law to be sin.

"Whosoever committeth sin transgresseth also the law: for sin is the transgression of the law" (1 John 3:4).

Sin is declared to be punishable by death. "The wages of sin is death" (Romans 6:23).

Thus it can be clearly seen that it was of supreme importance to know which was the seventh day. Not to know was to be in danger of violating the law of God. Thus would be incurred the penalty of death.

The Days of Creation

The days of the Bible are the same as the days we are familiar with, composed of a dark part called evening, or night, and a light part called morning, or day.

The days of Creation were not long periods of time, as many erroneously suppose, but covered the same length of time as our present days—an evening and a morning, or a dark part and a light part—as the earth revolved on its axis. This will be seen by the Divine Record: "God said, Let there be light: and there was light. And God saw the light, that it was good: and God divided the light from the darkness. And God called the light Day, and the darkness he called Night. And the evening and the morning were the first day" (Genesis 1:3-5).

Plainly, this was a literal day, with its evening and its morning, its dark part first and then the light part.

As the record of the Creation week continues, the work of each day closes with the statement, "The evening and the morning were the second day"; "the evening and the morning were the third day"; "the evening and the morning were the fourth day"; "the evening and the morning were the fifth day"; "the evening and the morning were the sixth day" (Genesis 1:8, 13, 19, 23, 31).

Literal Days

No other language could have been chosen by the inspired writer that would have made the thought of God more explicit than do these words. There are no other terms to be found in the Hebrew language that will express the idea of literal days more forcefully than the words here employed.

There was a first day, a second day, a third day, and on to the seventh day; each of these days opened and closed with a definite, literal evening and morning. The literal rendering of the Hebrew is, "There was evening, there was morning, day one"; "there was evening, there was morning, day two," and so on.

There is every reason to believe that the inspired penman of these words, Moses, the man of God, understood these days to mean, and intended his readers to understand them to mean, literal days. He certainly never had in mind anything similar to the ideas suggested by modern evolutionistic geology.

When Jehovah came down on Mount Sinai to give His law, He referred to these days of Creation as literal days, and intended the people so to understand them. The reason He gave for remembering the Sabbath day was that "in six days the Lord made heaven and earth, the sea, and all that in them is, and rested the seventh day." No unbiased mind can read these words and reach any conclusion other than that the *six days,* as well as the *seventh,* were literal days.

Nor is there any reason for seeking any other meaning. If God created the world, why could He not create it in six days? Why should He require a longer time than that to *speak* matter into existence? We are not grateful to those who, in order to relieve the record of seeming difficulties, have invented the purely theoretical and altogether visionary explanation of mighty periods of time. Such an explanation involves far more numerous and vastly more serious difficulties than those it seeks to avoid. We refuse to risk everything and gain nothing by forsaking the simple and natural and true interpretation of the scriptural record of Creation.

These, then, were real days, just as we know days now, not long ages, as evolutionists maintain.

Can the Original Seventh Day Be Found Now?

Then on the seventh day of the creative week, God did something different. On that day He "rested . . . from all his work which he had made." Then, because He had rested on the seventh day, "God blessed the seventh day, and sanctified it." (See Genesis 2:1-3.)

The question raised is: Can that blessed, holy, original rest day of the Creator now be found and located? There can be no doubt that it was given to mankind as a Sabbath, that it was indeed the Sabbath at that time, that God designed its observance by men to bring to them a blessing and to be a means of grace.

But can it now be found? Is it possible, through all the passing centuries and in spite of finite and changing calendars, positively to identify the original seventh day beyond any possibility of doubt?

Let this be set down at once and forever: God has not forgotten His holy day; He has not allowed it to become irrevocably lost, has not permitted its preservation to depend on the fallible reckoning of men, and is fully able to point it out infallibly to all those who are determined to fulfill His will.

An Institution as Old as History

There is an institution that has come down through the ages from the very earliest times to the present. That institution is known as the week. It is a period of time comprising seven days. It was known among the various nations and tribes of men in the ages of the past.

Every other period of time or grouping of the days together is marked by some movement of the heavenly bodies. This is not true of the week. There is no movement of heavenly bodies, of the sun, or moon, or stars, or planets, that determines the length of the week.

The year is marked by the time it takes the earth to complete one circuit of the sun. The month is marked by the revolution of the moon about the earth. The day is determined by the rotation of the earth on its axis.

But the period of the week is purely arbitrary, that is, there is nothing in nature suggesting such a grouping together of seven days. No celestial body circles the earth, or sun, or moon, or stars, or any planet, or is circled by these, in seven days.

The Origin of the Week

How, then, did the week originate? We will let the *Encyclopaedia Britannica* reply:

"The week is a period of seven days, having no reference whatever to the celestial motions—a circumstance to which it owes its unalterable uniformity. . . . It has been employed from time immemorial in almost all Eastern countries; and as it forms neither an aliquot part of the year nor of the lunar month, those who reject the Mosaic recital will be at a loss, as Delambre remarks, to assign to it an origin having much semblance of probability."—Eleventh edition, Vol. IV, p. 988, art. "Calendar."

Attention is also directed to the following observations from Thomas Hartwell Horne, in *an Introduction to the Critical Study and Knowledge of the Holy Scriptures:*

"One of the most striking collateral confirmations of the Mosaic history of the creation, is the general adoption of the

division of time into *weeks,* which extends from the Christian
states of Europe to the remote shores of Hindustan, and has
equally prevailed among the Hebrews, the Egyptians, Chi-
nese, Greeks, Romans, and northern barbarians—nations,
some of whom had little or no intercourse with others, and
were not even known by name to the Hebrews."—Edition of
1825, Vol. I, chap. 3, sec. 2, par. 1, p. 163.

Dr. Lyman Coleman remarks:

"Seven has been the ancient and honored number among
the nations of the earth. They have measured their time by
weeks from the beginning. The original of this was the Sabbath of God, as Moses has given the reasons for it in his writings."—*Brief Dissertations on the First Three Chapters of
Genesis,* p. 26.

Known From the Very Earliest Times

The Presbyterian Board of Publication, in its Tract No.
271, *The Christian Sabbath,* presents this:

"The division of time into weeks is not only *nonnatural,*
but in a sense *contranatural,* since the week of seven days is
no subdivision of either the naturally measured month or
year. Yet this singular measure of time by periods of seven
days may be traced not only through the sacred history before
the era of Moses, but in all ancient civilizations of every era,
many of which could not possibly have derived their notion
from Moses. . . . Among the learned of Egypt, the Brahmans
of India, by Arabs, by Assyrians, as may be gathered from
their astronomers and priests, this division was recognized.
Hesiod (900 B.C.) declares the seventh day is holy. So Homer
and Callimachus. Even in the Saxon mythology, the division
by weeks is prominent. Nay, even among the tribes of devil
worshipers in Africa, we are told that a peculiar feature of

their religion is a weekly sacred day, the violation of which by labor will incur the wrath of the devil god. Traces of a similar division of time have been noticed among the Indians of the American continent. Now, on what other theory are these facts explicable than upon the supposition of a divinely ordained Sabbath at the origin of the race?"—*Bound Tracts,* Vol. XII, pp. 5-7.

Seventh Day in Uninterrupted Succession

Alexander Campbell, the founder of the denomination known as the Christian Church, in his *Popular Lectures,* says this:

"Heaven left not this fact, the creation, the basis of a thousand volumes, to be gathered from abstract reasonings, vitiated traditions, ingenious analogies, or plausible conjectures, but from a *monumental* institution which was as *universal* as the annals of time, as the birth of nations, and as the languages spoken by mortals. An institution too, which, notwithstanding its demands, not only of the seventh part of all time, but of the *seventh day* in uninterrupted succession, was celebrated from the creation to the deluge, during the deluge, and after the deluge till the giving of the law."—Pages 283, 284.

The same writer, in his *Evidences of Christianity,* declares:

"The seventh day was observed from Abraham's time, nay, from creation."—Page 302.

The ancient Jewish historian, Josephus, in his book *Against Apion,* says:

"There is not any city of the Grecians, nor any of the barbarians, nor any nation whatsoever, whither our custom of resting on the seventh day hath not come."—Book 2, par. 40, in *Works of Flavius Josephus* (Winston ed.), p. 899.

R. M. ELDRIDGE, ARTIST

The identical Seventh-day Sabbath has come down to us all the way from Eden. It has never been "lost."

Since the Sabbath was set apart by God on the very first seventh day of earthly time, the period of the week was known from the very beginning.

It is also clear that the week was known by Noah at the time of the Flood.

"He stayed yet *other seven days;* and again he sent forth the dove out of the ark; and the dove came in to him in the evening; and, lo, in her mouth was an olive leaf plucked off: so Noah knew that the waters were abated from off the earth. And he stayed yet *other seven days;* and sent forth the dove; which returned not again unto him any more" (Genesis 8:10-12).

Now, what is it that determines in such an arbitrary manner, in the absence of any movement of the celestial bodies, this never-varying period of the week?

There is but one answer, and it is this: The never-failing recurrence every seven days of the Sabbath of the Lord.

This seventh-day Sabbath has been kept in unbroken succession through all the passing centuries. It was not lost before the days of Christ. It has not been lost since. It is not lost now. Jehovah, its Maker, has preserved it, and pointed it out to men as His Sabbath again and again.

More than twenty-five hundred years after Creation, God took occasion definitely to point out which was the original seventh day, and pointed it out in such a way that, even if there had been any confusion in the minds of His people before, none could remain when He had completed His identification of His holy day.

The record of what He did and how He identified the day —the literal, original seventh day—will be found in the sixteenth chapter of Exodus. It is the story of the falling of the manna in the wilderness.

Identical Seventh Day Pointed Out by God

"When the dew that lay was gone up, behold, upon the face of the wilderness there lay a small round thing, as small as the hoar frost on the ground. And when the children of Israel saw it, they said one to another, It is manna: for they wist not what it was.

"And Moses said unto them, This is the bread which the Lord hath given you to eat. This is the thing which the Lord hath commanded, Gather of it every man according to his eating, an omer for every man, according to the number of your persons; take ye every man for them which are in his tents.

"And the children of Israel did so, and gathered, some more, some less. And when they did mete it with an omer, he that gathered much had nothing over, and he that gathered little had no lack; they gathered every man according to his eating. And Moses said, Let no man leave of it till the morning. Notwithstanding they hearkened not unto Moses; but some of them left of it until the morning, and it bred worms, and stank: and Moses was wroth with them. And they gathered it every morning . . . : and when the sun waxed hot, it melted.

"And it came to pass, that on the sixth day they gathered twice as much bread, two omers for one man: and all the rulers of the congregation came and told Moses. And he said unto them, This is that which the Lord hath said, To morrow is the rest of the holy sabbath unto the Lord. . . . And they laid it up till the morning, as Moses bade: and it did not stink, neither was there any worm therein.

"And Moses said, Eat that to day; for to day is a sabbath unto the Lord: to day ye shall not find it in the field. Six days ye shall gather it; but on the seventh day, which is the sabbath, in it there shall be none.

"And it came to pass, that there went out some of the people on the seventh day for to gather, and they found none. And the Lord said unto Moses, How long refuse ye to keep my commandments and my laws? See, for that the Lord hath given you the sabbath, therefore he giveth you on the sixth day the bread of two days; abide ye every man in his place, let no man go out of his place on the seventh day. So the people rested on the seventh day" (Exodus 16:14-30).

Here the identical seventh day is pointed out by God, without reference to the calendars of men and without any need of consulting human records. The Maker of the days, the Creator of the heavenly bodies, the Master of time and eternity, deigns to point out to His fallible, erring creatures which is His day, the identical seventh day of Creation. There was no possibility of any mistake about it. No one could truthfully say he could not find the day. It was so plain now that no one could lose it.

Three Distinct Weekly Miracles Identified the Day

By three distinct miracles God identified the seventh day: He gave twice as much manna as usual on the sixth day; He kept that manna unspoiled overnight, whereas on all other nights it spoiled and could not be kept; and on the seventh day, the identical seventh day of Creation, God's day, the blessed Sabbath, He withheld all manna from falling.

And these three miracles were repeated every week, fifty-two weeks a year, for forty years, during the wandering of the Israelites in the wilderness.

That is, 2,500 years this side of Creation the Lord of the Sabbath Himself took occasion to point out about 2,080 identical seventh days in order that there need be no mistake about the identity of the Sabbath.

No, the seventh-day Sabbath is not difficult to find. On the contrary, it is impossible to lose.

The Israelites have continued to observe that identical day, thus pointed out, through all the passing centuries, without ever since losing it or becoming confused regarding it. That observance has been unbroken from that time to this. They entered into an oath to walk in God's law, especially in respect to Sabbathkeeping.

"They . . . entered into a curse, and into an oath, to walk in God's law, . . . and to observe and do all the commandments of the Lord our Lord, and his judgments and his statutes; . . . and if the people of the land bring ware or any victuals on the sabbath day to sell, that we would not buy it of them on the sabbath" (Nehemiah 10:29-31).

They did not have the Gregorian calendar that we have. They did not need it in order to count seven. At the end of every seven-day period they observed the holy Sabbath.

Sabbath Not Altered by Changes in Calendars

Calendars have changed, but the week has never been broken from the beginning of time. Regardless of all systems of reckoning time, in spite of changes from one calendar to another, notwithstanding all the inaccuracies of men, the week stretches in unbroken succession back to the very beginning when God called His creation into existence. You cannot lose the Sabbath. Its occurrence and recurrence do not depend on the shifting calculations of men, but on the omnipotent power and omniscient wisdom of the Lord our God.

Coming down four thousand years this side of Creation, we once more find the identical seventh day definitely pointed out, this time in the New Testament. It is the occasion of the crucifixion and resurrection of our Lord. This is the record:

"This man [Joseph of Arimathaea] went unto Pilate, and begged the body of Jesus. And he took it down, and wrapped it in linen, and laid it in a sepulchre that was hewn in stone, wherein never man before was laid. And *that day* was the preparation, and the sabbath drew on. And the women also, which came with him from Galilee, followed after, and beheld the sepulchre, and how his body was laid. And they returned, and prepared spices and ointments; and rested *the sabbath day according to the commandment.* Now upon *the first day of the week,* very early in the morning, they came unto the sepulchre, bringing the spices which they had prepared, and certain others with them. And they found the stone rolled away from the sepulchre" (Luke 23:52 to 24:2).

Here the day on which the crucifixion took place, which is known to have been Friday, or the sixth day of the week, is given a name, "the preparation." The next day, the seventh, the day upon which the Lord of life rested in the tomb, is positively identified as "the sabbath day according to the commandment," the identical seventh day of Creation. The next day, the first day of the week, upon which our Lord was raised from the dead, is not given a name, either sacred or secular, but is spoken of merely as "the first day of the week."

In this passage, then, three days are brought before us, and their relation to one another is clearly revealed. The Sabbath day, even "the sabbath day according to the commandment," is seen, even in the New Testament, to be the day between the sixth day, Friday, and the first day, now known as Sunday. That is, Sunday is not, and never has been, the Sabbath of the New Testament. That Sabbath, the true Sabbath of God, "the sabbath day according to the commandment," is the day immediately before Sunday. When Sunday begins, the true Sabbath is past.

No Possibility of Losing the Sabbath

At that very time Sunday was being observed by sun worshipers. Later, through apostasy and departure from God, the observance of Sunday was brought into the church. It was never brought in by divine authority, and its observance is no part of true Christianity.

So also at that time the seventh day was observed by the Jews. The first day was observed by sun worshipers. Both of these days, the seventh and the first, have been kept in unbroken succession ever since, the seventh day by the Jews and Sabbathkeeping Christians, the first day by sun worshipers, and later by Sundaykeeping Christians. These two days, having been so observed, have come down to us in unbroken line, being kept week after week through all the Christian centuries, without possibility of being lost.

Thus we can trace the Sabbath through all the years stretching between Creation and now. It has not been lost. There has been no change in it. It is the same Sabbath now as it was when it came from the hand of God. It was made of the seventh day. It is still the seventh day. Again I say, so far from being unable to find the seventh day, the fact is we are unable to lose it.

But, it is asked, has not the calendar been changed many times, and have not such changes resulted in changing the Sabbath? This, too, we shall study.

The Change
of the Calendar

THE Gregorian calendar, now in use throughout the world, is precise and accurate. It will be helpful as we begin the study of the changes that brought about its adoption for the reader to place a copy of this calendar before his eyes for careful observation. Yes, it is the one you have hanging on the wall.

Look particularly at the order of the days of the week. Sunday is the first day, Monday the second, Tuesday the third, Wednesday the fourth, Thursday the fifth, Friday the sixth, and Saturday the seventh.

The names given these days are all pagan in their origin. Sunday was named for the sun, the sun's day; Monday for the moon; Tuesday for the goddess Tiw; Wednesday for the ancient Germanic war god, Woden; Thursday for the old Norse god of thunder, Thor; Friday for the goddess Frigga; and Saturday for the god Saturn. The old Latin names for these days in their order are as follows: *Dies Solis, Dies Lunae, Dies Martis, Dies Mercurii, Dies Jovis, Dies Veneris, Dies Saturni,* these names being given in honor of the sun, the moon, Mars, Mercury, Jove, Venus, and Saturn, respectively.

It is a common impression that many changes of the calendar have taken place between Christ's time and ours. This is not true. There has been but one, the change from the Julian calendar to the Gregorian. And that change had no effect whatever upon the days of the week. There has been no change in the days of the week since the time of Christ, nor was there any change before that, so far as records show. The days of the month were changed in the adoption of the Gregorian calendar, but not the days of the week. They have remained unchanged from the beginning and are the same now as in all past history.

The calendar that was used in Palestine and in all the provinces of the Roman Empire in the days of Christ was known as the Julian calendar. It came into use by the authority and in the time of Julius Caesar, and is named after him. It was promulgated in the 708th year of the city of Rome, about 46 B.C.

Julius Caesar loved to be prominent. He took to himself many prerogatives. He named the seventh month after himself, and to this day it is known as July, after Julius. It is said that in choosing a month to name after himself, he was careful to choose one with thirty-one days, as he considered his name worthy of one of the longest months in the year. The next month at that time contained thirty days. Augustus Caesar, the successor of Julius, accounted himself of not one whit less importance than Julius, and when he named August after himself, he added to it another day, which he took from February, so that it would contain as many days as July.

Julian Calendar Not Accurate

The Julian calendar was used for fifteen centuries after Christ in practically the entire civilized world. It was not, however, an accurate calendar. It assumed the length of the solar year to be 365¼ days, whereas it is eleven minutes and a few seconds less than that. This does not seem to be a great error, but in the course of years it accumulated. As a result, under the Julian calendar a little time was lost each year; that is, it was not based exactly on the movements of the celestial bodies, and the result was that, year by year, the vernal equinox, which in Julius Caesar's time occurred about March 25, gradually receded toward the first of March. By the beginning of the sixteenth century after Christ it was occurring about March 11.

As long ago as the thirteenth century, astronomers began to write about the inaccuracy of the Julian calendar. Some of the countries of Europe desired to take action looking toward a reform of the calendar. But nothing was done for a long time, because leadership and agreement were necessary in order to establish a revision of the calendar that would bring about uniformity in all countries.

From Julian to Gregorian

At last the sympathy and interest of the Papacy itself were enlisted. Under Pope Gregory XIII the calendar was changed, and a correction of ten days was made to bring back March 21 to the vernal equinox, where it had stood at the time of the Council of Nicaea in 325 when the question of Easter celebration was settled by that church council. (See *Catholic Encyclopedia,* Vol. III, pp. 168, 169, art. "Calendar, Reform of the.") He published a bull, dated March 1, 1582, annulling ten days, so that the day which would have been reckoned the 5th of October, 1582, was to be reckoned the 15th of October. The new calendar was given the name of the pope in whose pontificate the new calendar was established, Pope Gregory. It is therefore known as the Gregorian calendar.

The Gregorian calendar, which you now use in your

Julius Caesar   Gregory XIII

1582	OCTOBER				1582	
SUN	MON	TUE	WED	THU	FRI	SAT
	1	2	3	4	15	16
17	18	19	20	21	22	23
24	25	26	27	28	29	30
31						

When the Julian calendar was corrected by Pope Gregory in 1582, ten days were dropped from the calendar count, as is shown here. What would have been Friday the 5th became Friday the 15th. The continuity of the days of the week was not altered or interrupted, nor has it been in any calendar change.

home, and according to which nearly all the world reckons time, was, as has been said, established by proclamation of the pope of Rome in A.D. 1582. The change that put it into effect, a change of ten days between it and the old Julian calendar, was made on Friday, October 5, 1582. The way the ten days were made up was merely to call that day, which under the Julian calendar was the 5th of October, the 15th of October. This is all that was done. And this made the calendar year uniform with the vernal equinox.

No Difference in the Sabbath

The day was still Friday, but instead of being Friday the 5th, it was Friday the 15th. There was no difference in the month. It was still October. There was no difference in the week. There was no difference in the day of the week. It was still Friday. The difference was in the day of the month. It was the 15th instead of the 5th. That is all.

The next day was Saturday, just as it would have been if the calendar had not been changed. Only it was the sixteenth instead of the sixth. The change of the calendar made no change in the Sabbath of the Lord, and creates no difficulty in locating the identical seventh day now.

Spain, Portugal, and Italy adopted the new Gregorian calendar at once. A little later in the same year, 1582, France adopted it, by calling the 10th of December the 20th. The Catholic states of Germany adopted the new calendar in the year 1583, but in the Protestant states of Germany the old style, or Julian calendar, was adhered to until the year 1700. In that year the Low Countries, as they were called, or the Netherlands, adopted the new calendar. They were not friendly to the Papacy, and hence were slow to accept anything that they considered came from the pope.

England did not adopt the new calendar until the year 1752. Sweden and Denmark accepted it about the same time as the Protestant states of Germany.

Days Identically the Same Under Both Calendars

During all this time when some of the countries were reckoning time under one calendar and some under another, the days of the week were identically the same in all countries. When it was Saturday in Spain and Portugal and Italy, it was also Saturday in England, although until the year 1700 they were ten days apart in their dates, and after 1700 they were eleven days apart.

England had refused to accept the new calendar because at that time she was passing through the experience of establishing what has later come to be known as the Church of England, and wanted nothing whatever to do with the Papacy. The difference in the reckoning of dates, however, resulted in confusion and difficulty in the transaction of business between England and the Continent. Finally the businessmen of England made such an agitation over the matter that England was obliged to adopt the new calendar, which by that time was known to be accurate and precise.

In the study of history one will often observe, when dates of certain events are referred to, the letters "O.S." or "N.S." They are for the purpose of indicating whether the old style or new style calendar is referred to.

Date Changed, but Not the Day

It was on September 2, 1752, that the new style calendar, the Gregorian, was adopted by the British Parliament. The act of Parliament reads merely that the day following September 2 should be called September 14. The day was Thursday. Under the old style, or Julian calendar, it would have been Thursday the 3d. The act of Parliament adopting the Gregorian calendar made it Thursday the 14th. The difference between the old style and the new style by that time amounted to eleven days. The second of September was followed by the 14th of September. The day of the month was changed but not the day of the week. The 2d was Wednesday. The next day, the 14th, was Thursday. It would have been Thursday if the change had not been made. But it would have been Thursday the 3d; now it was Thursday the 14th. Following this was Friday the 15th, then Saturday the 16th. If the change had not been made, this Saturday would have been the 5th of September. But it would still have been Saturday. It was the seventh day of the week on the Continent; it was the seventh day in England; it was the seventh day everywhere. The dates attached to that day had been different on the Continent and in England. Now they were made the same. But the day was not changed. The day was not lost. There was no confusion in the matter. The change made did not affect the days of the week at all. They continued and remained just the same.

From 1582, when the new style calendar had been adopted in Italy, to 1752, when it was adopted in Great Britain, is 170 years. During all these 170 years, when countries of the Continent of Europe were using the new style calendar, England had been using the old style calendar. At one time they were ten days apart in their reckoning, at a later time eleven days. But during all this time the days of the week were just the same on the Continent as they were in England. There was no confusion at all concerning them. Certainly this is conclusive evidence that the change in the calendar made no difference in the days of the week.

Under Different Calendars, but With the Same Days

Russia and Greece continued using the old style calendar. They were under the influence of the Greek Church, which was not in communion with the see of Rome; hence they would not adopt the new calendar. Rumania, Serbia, and Turkey, however, finally adopted the Gregorian calendar in 1919, and Soviet Russia made the change soon after the revolution. In none of these changes were the days of the week affected. By that time the difference between the two calendars amounted to fourteen days.

While the *dates* in Germany were not the same as the dates in Russia, the *days* were just the same. When it was Monday in Russia it was Monday in Germany, though they were under different calendars. When the Sabbath came in Germany, the seventh day of the week, it was Sabbath in Russia as well, though the dates on the calendar were fourteen days apart. What the *Encyclopaedia Britannica* called the "unalterable uniformity" of the week has never been affected by calendar changes. Hence the day of the Sabbath has not been changed or altered or affected in the slightest degree by such changes.

So do not permit anyone to confuse your thinking by talking about the change of the calendar. Those who really know how that change was made realize that the adoption of the new calendar did not in any way affect the days of the week. Indeed, the calendar is itself one of the best means of confirming the definiteness of the identical seventh day of Creation.

The Identical Seventh Day of Creation

We believe the Bible is true. The Bible commands the observance of the seventh day of the week. That identical seventh day can be found if anyone wants to find it. And it can be found even if anyone wants to lose it. There is no way by which it can be lost. When the sun goes down on Friday night, the identical seventh day of Creation begins. It is the identical seventh day that God's command charges us to keep. That command declares, "The seventh day is the sabbath of the Lord thy God: in it thou shalt not do any work." Therefore, when the sun sets this coming Friday night, you will be in holy time.

© 1949, BY REVIEW AND HERALD

RUSSELL HARLAN, ARTIST

Jesus Christ consistently upheld His Father's law and practiced true Sabbathkeeping while He was here.
on earth

The Position of Protestantism

THE position of Protestantism with reference to the Sabbath is greatly confused. Multitudes of voices are raised, discussing all sides of the question and advancing arguments that are mutually destructive.

From an examination of the official teachings of the various denominations of Protestantism, it becomes apparent that Protestant Christians, in observing Sunday, are engaging in a practice for which there is no defense in valid Protestant teaching, and which, if the Protestant principle of "the Bible and the Bible only" is adhered to, must be discarded. Unfortunately, Protestant practice is not always in accord with Protestant teaching.

Protestantism began as a protest against the corruptions of Romanism and appealed to the Bible as the sole authority in matters of Christian faith and practice. Chillingworth, in his famous statement, set forth the Protestant platform in words that have been, ought to be, and are endorsed by all true Protestants. He said:

The Bible, and the Bible Only

"The Bible, I say, the Bible only, is the religion of Protestants! . . . I for my part, after a long and (as I verily believe and hope) impartial search of 'the true way to eternal happiness,' do profess plainly that I cannot find any rest for the sole of my foot but upon this rock only. I see plainly and with mine own eyes that there are popes against popes, councils against councils, some Fathers against others, the same Fathers against themselves, a consent of the Fathers of one age against a consent of the Fathers of another age. . . .

"There is no sufficient certainty but of Scripture only for any considering man to build upon. This, therefore, and this only, I have reason to believe: this I will profess; according to this I will live, and for this, if there be occasion, I will not only willingly, but even gladly, lose my life, though I should be sorry that Christians should take it from me. Propose me anything out of this Book, and require whether I believe it or no, and seem it never so incomprehensible to human reason, I will subscribe it with hand and heart, as knowing no demonstration can be stronger than this: God hath said so, therefore it is true."—*The Religion of Protestants a Safe Way to Salvation* (1846), p. 463.

Dr. John Dowling, who for many years was pastor of the Berean Baptist church in New York City, wrote a *History of Romanism,* in which he repeated this statement of Chillingworth's, and then went on to add the following:

" 'The Bible, I say, the Bible only, is the religion of Protestants!' Nor is it of any account in the estimation of the genuine Protestant *how early* a doctrine originated, if it is not found in the Bible. . . . Hence if a doctrine be propounded for his acceptance, he asks, Is it to be found in the Inspired Word? Was it taught by the Lord Jesus Christ and His apostles? If they knew nothing of it, no matter to him whether it be discovered in the musty folio of some ancient visionary of the third or fourth century, or whether it spring from the fertile brain of some modern visionary of the nineteenth, if it is not found in the Sacred Scriptures, it presents no valid claim to be received as an article of his religious creed. . . . He who receives a single doctrine upon the mere authority of tradition, let him be called by what name he will, by so doing, steps down from the Protestant rock, passes over the line which separates Protestantism from popery, and can give no valid reason why he should not receive all the earlier doctrines and ceremonies of Romanism, upon the same authority."—Thirteenth edition, pp. 67, 68.

In the light of this great and true principle we direct attention to the practice of Protestant people in observing the first day of the week instead of the true Sabbath of God, which is the seventh day. How are these things to be reconciled?

Ten Commandments Not Abolished

There are some religious teachers today who claim that the Ten Commandment law has been nullified, abolished, set aside, nailed to the cross by Christ, and therefore that no Christian is under obligation to keep the Sabbath. Not even their own denominational faith will justify them in such a claim, to say nothing of the clear teaching of the Holy Scriptures. The official teaching of the various Protestant bodies regarding the perpetuity of the law of God is set forth in clear pronouncements in their manuals, disciplines, confessions of faith, and in the words of their recognized leaders. Not one of them, so far as we have record, takes the position that God's law has been set aside and is no longer binding upon men. Indeed, their united testimony is to the exact contrary.

In both the Church of England and the Protestant Episcopal Church in the United States it is customary for the minister, in celebrating the Lord's Supper, to recite the Ten Com-

mandments, and for the people, in response, at the conclusion
of each commandment, to say, "Lord, have mercy upon us and
incline our hearts to keep this law." Certainly these branches
of Protestantism do not officially teach that the Ten Commandment law has been set aside.

The Law "Eternal and Unchangeable"

The official teaching of the Baptist denomination is set
forth in the *New Hampshire Confession of Faith,* and there
certainly is no teaching of the abolition, or even of the altera-
tion, of God's law in this strong statement:

"We believe the Scriptures teach that the law of God is
the eternal and unchangeable rule of His moral government;
that it is holy, just, and good; and that the inability which the
Scriptures ascribe to fallen men to fulfill its precepts arises
entirely from their love of sin; to deliver them from which, and
to restore them through a Mediator to unfeigned obedience to
the holy law, is one great end of the gospel, and of the means
of grace connected with the establishment of the visible
church."—Article 12, quoted in O. C. S. WALLACE, *What
Baptists Believe* (1934), p. 79.

Disowning the Law Subverts the Gospel

That Christians, because they have greater light, are under
greater obligation to observe the precepts of the law than any
others, is emphasized by the Baptist Publication Society in its
Tract No. 64, which declares:

"To prove that the ten commandments are binding, let any
person read them, one by one, and ask his own conscience as
he reads, whether it would be any sin to break them. Is this, or
any part of it, the liberty of the gospel? Every conscience that

is not seared as with a hot iron must answer these questions in the negative . . . The lawgiver and the Saviour were one; and believers must be of one mind with the former as well as with the latter; but if we depreciate the law which Christ delighted to honor, and deny our obligations to obey it, how are we of His mind? Rather are we not of that mind which is emnity against God, which is not subject to the law of God, neither indeed can be? . . . If the law be not a rule of conduct to believers, and a perfect rule too, they are under no rule; or, which is the same thing, are lawless. But if so, they commit no sin; for *where no law is there is no transgression;* and in this case they have no sins to confess, either to God or to one another; nor do they stand in need of Christ as an advocate with the Father, nor of daily forgiveness through His blood. Thus it is, by disowning the law, men utterly subvert the gospel. Believers, therefore, instead of being freed from obligation to obey it, are under greater obligation to do so than any men in the world. To be exempt from this is to be without law, and of course without sin; in which case we might do without a Saviour, which is utterly subversive of all religion."—Pages 2-6.

Grace and Atonement Rendered Void by Antinomianism

The Reverend Andrew Fuller, an eminent Baptist minister known as "the Franklin of theology," says:

"If the doctrine of the atonement leads us to entertain degrading notions of the law of God, or to plead an exemption from its preceptive authority, we may be sure it is not the Scripture doctrine of reconciliation. Atonement has respect to justice, and justice to the law, or the revealed will of the Sovereign, which has been violated; and the very design of the atonement is to repair the honor of the law. If the law which has been transgressed were unjust, instead of an atonement being required for the breach of it, it ought to have been repealed, and the Lawgiver have taken upon Himself the disgrace of having enacted it. . . . It is easy to see from hence, that in proportion as the law is depreciated, the gospel is undermined, and both grace and atonement rendered void. It is the law as abused, or as turned into a way of life, in opposition to the gospel, for which it was never given to a fallen creature, that the Sacred Scriptures depreciate it; and not as the revealed will of God, the immutable standard of right and wrong. In this view the apostles delighted in it; and if we are Christians, we shall delight in it too, and shall not object to be under it as a rule of duty; for no man objects to be governed by laws which he loves."—"Atonement of Christ," in *Works of Andrew Fuller,* pp. 160, 161.

Incomparable Perfection Proof of Law's Divinity

Charles Spurgeon, that prince of Baptist preachers, in his *Perpetuity of the Law of God,* says:

"Jesus did not come to change the law, but He came to explain it, and that very fact shows that it remains; for there is no need to explain that which is abrogated. . . . By thus explaining the law He confirmed it; He could not have meant to abolish it, or He would not have needed to expound it. . . . That the Master did not come to alter the law is clear, because after having embodied it in His life, He willingly gave Himself up to bear its penalty, though He had never broken it, bearing the penalty for us, even as it is written, 'Christ hath redeemed us from the curse of the law, being made a curse for us.' . . . If the law had demanded more of us than it ought to have done, would the Lord Jesus have rendered to it the penalty which resulted from its too severe demands? I am sure He would not. But because the law asked only what it ought to ask, namely, perfect obedience, and exacted of the transgressor only what it ought to exact, namely, death as the penalty for sin—death under divine wrath—therefore the Saviour went to the tree, and there bore our sins, and purged them once for all."—Pages 4-7.

Again, in his *Sermons,* Spurgeon says:

"The law of God is a divine law, holy, heavenly, perfect. . . . There is not a commandment too many; there is not one too few; but it is so *incomparable* that its *perfection* is a proof of its divinity. No human lawgiver could have given forth such a law as that which we find in the decalogue."—VOL. II, Sermon 18, p. 280.

Methodism Upholds the Law

Turning now to the official teaching of the Methodist Episcopal Church, we find that great community of Christians thus upholding the obligation to observe the law of God:

"Although the law given from God by Moses as touching ceremonies and rites, doth not bind Christians, nor ought the civil precepts thereof of necessity be received in any commonwealth; yet, notwithstanding, no Christian whatsoever is free from the obedience of the commandments which are called moral."—Constitution of the Methodist Episcopal Church, "Articles of Religion," Art. 6, in *Methodist Episcopal Church Doctrines and Discipline* (1928), p. 7.

The father of Methodism, John Wesley, had much to say regarding the law of God, and the duty of Christians to observe it. He strongly defended it against those who taught its abolition. We direct particular attention to the statements that follow, all taken from his writings:

"The moral law contained in the ten commandments, and enforced by the prophets, He [Christ] did not take away. It was not the design of His coming to revoke any part of this. This is the law which never can be broken, which 'stands fast as the faithful witness in heaven.' The moral law stands on an entirely different foundation from the ceremonial or ritual law. . . . Every part of the law must remain in force upon all mankind, and in all ages; as not depending either on time or place, or any other circumstances liable to change, but on the nature of God and the nature of man, and their unchangeable relation to each other."—"On the Sermon on the Mount," Discourse 6, *Sermons on Several Occasions* (1810), pp. 75, 76.

Wesley on the Perpetuity of the Law

From the same sermon we take these statements:

"In the highest rank of the enemies of the gospel of Christ, are they who, openly and explicitly, 'judge the law,' itself, and 'speak evil of the law'; who teach men to break (*lusai, to dissolve, to loose, to untie* the obligation of) not one only, whether of the least, or of the greatest, but all the commandments at a stroke; who teach, without any cover, in so many words, 'What did our Lord do with the law? He abolished it. There is but one duty, which is that of believing. . . .' This is indeed carrying matters with a high hand; this is withstanding our Lord to the face, and telling Him, that He understood not how to deliver the message on which He was sent. O Lord, lay not this sin to their charge! Father, forgive them; for they know not what they do!

"The most surprising of all the circumstances, that attend this strong delusion is, that they who are given up to it really believe, that they honor Christ, by overthrowing His law, and that they are magnifying His office, while they are destroying His doctrine! Yea, they honor Him just as Judas did, when he said, 'Hail, Master, and kissed Him.' And He may as justly, say to every one of them, 'Betrayest thou the Son of man with a kiss?' It is no other than betraying Him with a kiss, to talk of His blood and take away His crown; to set light by any part of His law, under pretense of advancing His gospel. Nor indeed can anyone escape this charge, who preaches faith in any such a manner, as either directly or indirectly tends to set aside any branch of obedience; who preaches Christ so as to disannul, or weaken in any wise, the least of the commandments of God."—*Ibid.,* pp. 81, 82.

Gospel Without Significance Except as Based on Law

Bishop Matthew Simpson, of the Methodist Episcopal Church, delivered the Yale Lectures on Preaching in the year 1878, which later were published by Eton and Mains under the title *Lectures on Preaching.* In his fourth lecture Bishop Simpson said:

"The law of God . . . should be distinctly set forth. Our congregations should be gathered as around the base of Mount Sinai, while from its summit is heard the voice of God in those commandments which are unalterable and eternal in their character. . . . There are many preachers who love to dwell on the gospel alone. . . . But sometimes they go beyond this, and declaim against the preaching of the law—intimate that it belongs to a past age, a less civilized society; that men can best be moved by love alone. . . . Such a gospel may rear a beautiful structure; but its foundation is on the sand. No true edifice can be raised without its foundations' being dug deep by repentance toward God. . . . The law without the gospel is dark and hopeless; the gospel without law is inefficient and powerless. The one leads to servitude, the other to anti-nomianism. The two combined produce 'charity out of a pure heart, and of a good conscience, and of faith unfeigned.' "—Pages 128, 129.

Law Can Never Become Obsolete

In the Methodist Episcopal *Catechism,* Numbers 1 and 2, is this catechetical instruction:

"*Ques.*—What does God require of man?

"*Ans.*—Obedience to His revealed will.

"*Ques.*—What is the rule of our obedience?

"*Ans.*—The moral law.

"*Ques.*—Where is the moral law given?

"*Ans.*—In the ten commandments.

"*Ques.*—Are all Christians under obligation to keep the law?

"*Ans.*—Yes."—Number 2, pp. 38, 43; Number 1, p. 18.

Bishop E. O. Haven, also of the Methodist Episcopal Church, and one-time president of Michigan University, said:

"This decalogue can never become obsolete. It was de-signed for all men, and, obeyed, would render all men noble and worthy of immortal blessedness. It is a kind of consecration of the moral teachings of the Bible."—*Pillars of Truth,* p. 235.

Christ Strengthened Obligation to Keep the Law

The Presbyterian denomination is not a whit behind these others in loyalty to God's ten commandments. Article V of the Presbyterian *Confession of Faith* declares thus positively:

"The moral law doth forever bind all, as well justified persons as others, to the obedience thereof; and that not only in regard of the matter contained in it, but also in respect of the authority of God the Creator who gave it. Neither doth Christ in the gospel in any way dissolve, but much strengthen, this obligation."—Chapter 19, sec. 5, in *The Constitution of the Presbyterian Church in the United States of America* (1896), pp. 88, 89.

Eternal Rule of a Devout and Holy Life

The great Reformer, John Calvin, commenting on Matthew 5:17 and Luke 16:17, in his *Commentary on a Harmony of the Gospels,* says:

"We must not imagine that the coming of Christ has freed us from the authority of the law; for it is the eternal rule of a devout and holy life, and must, therefore, be as unchangeable as the justice of God, which it embraced, is constant and uniform."—Volume I, p. 277.

In his *Institutes* Calvin wrote:

"The law sustained no diminution of its authority, but ought always to receive from us the same veneration and obedience."—ii. 7, sec. 15.

Jesus Neither Abolished nor Superseded the Ten Commandments

Dr. Albert Barnes, the noted Presbyterian commentator, in his comments on Matthew 5:18, says:

"The laws of the Jews are commonly divided into moral, ceremonial, and judicial. The moral laws are such as grow out of the *nature of things,* which cannot, therefore, be changed—such as the duty of loving God and His creatures. These cannot be abolished, as it can never be made right to *hate* God, or to hate our fellow men. Of this kind are the ten commandments; and these our Saviour has neither abolished nor superseded."—*Notes, Explanatory and Practical, on the Gospels* (1860 ed.), Vol. I, p. 65.

Commenting on Matthew 5:19, the same writer says:

"We learn hence: 1. That all the law of God is binding on Christians. Compare James 2:10. 2. That all the commands of God should be preached, in their proper place, by Christian ministers. 3. That they who pretend that there are any laws of God so small that they need not obey them, are unworthy of His kingdom. And 4. That true piety has respect to *all* the commandments of God. Compare Ps. 119:6."—*Ibid.*, p. 66.

Timothy Dwight a Congregationalist, declares:

"The law of God is and must of necessity be unchangeable and eternal."—*Theology,* Vol. IV, p. 120.

Jonathan Edwards, the great Congregationalist preacher and one-time president of Princeton University, in *The Works of Jonathan Edwards,* says:

"Through the atonement of Christ more honor is done to the law, and consequently the law is more established, than if the law had been literally executed, and all mankind had been condemned. Whatever tends most to the honor of the law, tends most to establish its authority."—Edition of 1842, Vol. II, p. 369.

Christ Made the Law All the More Searching

Dwight L. Moody, the great revivalist, in his *Weighed and Wanting,* makes these statements:

"Now men may cavil as much as they like about other parts of the Bible, but I have never met an honest man that found fault with the ten commandments. Infidels may mock the Lawgiver and reject Him who has delivered us from the curse of the law, but they can't help admitting that the commandments are right. Renan said that they are for all nations, and will remain the commandments of God during all the centuries."

"The people must be made to understand that the ten commandments are still binding, and that there is a penalty attached to their violation."

"The commandments of God given to Moses in the mount at Horeb are as binding today as ever they have been since the time when they were proclaimed in the hearing of the people. The Jews said the law was not given in Palestine (which belonged to Israel), but in the wilderness, because the law was for all nations."

"Jesus never condemned the law and the prophets, but He did condemn those who did not obey Him. Because He gave new commandments, it does not follow that He abolished the old. Christ's explanation of them made them all the more searching."—Pages 11, 16, 15.

Of Universal Application

The position of the Lutheran Church may be stated in the words of one of its modern catechisms:

"23. *How many kinds of laws did God give in the Old Testament?*

"Three kinds: 1. The ceremonial church law; 2. The civil law; 3. The moral law.

"24. *Which of these laws is still in force?*

"The moral law, which is contained in the ten commandments.

"25. *Cannot this law be abolished?*

"No; because it is founded on God's holy and righteous nature."—*Epitome of Pontoppidan's "Explanation of Martin Luther's Small Catechism"* (1935), pp. 6, 7.

In his "Against the Antinomians," Luther observes:

"I wonder exceedingly how it came to be imputed to me that I should reject the law of ten commandments. . . . Can anyone think that sin exists where there is no law? Whoever abrogates the law, must of necessity abrogate sin also." —Translated from *Luther's Works* (Weimar ed.), vol. 50, pp. 470, 471.

In M. Michelet's *Life of Luther* he is quoted as saying:

"He who destroys the doctrine of the law, destroys at the same time political and social order. If you eject the law from the church, there will no longer be any sin recognized as such in the world; for the gospel only defines and punishes sin by reference to the law."—v. 4, Hazlitt's tr. (2d ed.), p. 315.

The position of the Free Methodist Church may be seen from the *Free Methodist Discipline,* which in its fifth article reads:

"No Christian whatsoever is free from the obedience of the commandments which are called moral."

Alexander Campbell may be taken as the spokesman of the Christian Church. In his debate with Purcell he said:

"God's ten words, . . . not only in the Old Testament, but in all revelation, are the most emphatically regarded as the synopsis of all religion and morality."—*Debate on the Roman Catholic Religion,* p. 214.

Smith's Dictionary of the Bible declares:

"Though even the decalogue is affected by the New Testament, it is not so in the way of repeal or obliteration. It is raised, transfigured, glorified there, but itself remains in its authority and supremacy."—Edition of 1863, Vol. III, p. 1071.

In Buck's Theological Dictionary, in its article on "Law," there are these statements:

"Moral law is that declaration of God's will which directs and binds all men, in every age and place, to their whole duty to Him. It was most solemnly proclaimed by God Himself at Sinai. . . . It is denominated perfect (Psalms 19:7), perpetual (Matthew 5:17, 18), holy (Romans 7:12), good (Romans 7:12), spiritual (Romans 7:14), exceeding broad (Psalms 119:96)."—Page 230.

Limitations of space prevent the addition of more quotations regarding the law. All Protestant denominations, however, agree that God's ten commandment law is still to be observed by Christians; that it is an eternal and unchangeable standard of righteousness; and that the obligation to keep its precepts has been strengthened by Christ rather than lessened or done away.

Notwithstanding this formal and official acceptance and endorsement of the law, however, the members of these communions uniformly observe a day that is never once mentioned in the Ten Commandments, and as uniformly neglect and ignore the observance of the day that is there positively and pointedly commanded.

Admit the Sabbath Has Remained Unchanged

Is this failure to live up to their own profession due to a sincere belief that that part of the law which commands the observance of the seventh day has been done away, while all the rest remains in force? No, not at all, for these same denominations are just as emphatic regarding the fourth commandment as they are concerning the rest. This is apparent from their own writings, which are here given.

Writing on the way in which Sunday observance crept into the practice of Christians, Archdeacon Farrar (Church of England), in his *The Voice From Sinai*, says:

"The Christian church made no formal, but a gradual and almost unconscious transference of the one day to the other."
—Page 167.

Dr. Peter Heylyn (Church of England), in his *History of the Sabbath,* says:

"Take which you will, either the Fathers or the moderns, and we shall find no Lord's day instituted by any apostolical mandate, no Sabbath set on foot by them upon the first day of the week."—Part 2, chap. 1, p. 28.

Bishop Jeremy Taylor, also of the Church of England, in his *Ductor Dubitantium,* writes:

"The Lord's day did not succeed in the place of the Sabbath, but the Sabbath was wholly abrogated, and the Lord's day was merely of ecclesiastical institution. It was not introduced by virtue of the fourth commandment, because they for almost three hundred years together kept that day which was in that commandment." "The primitive Christians did all manner of works upon the Lord's day, even in the times of persecution, when they are the strictest observers of all the divine commandments; but in this they knew there was none."—Part 1, ii. 2, rule 6, secs. 51, 59 (1850 ed.), Vol. IX, pp. 458, 464.

Into the Rest of Sunday No Divine Law Enters

Canon Eyton (Church of England), in his *Ten Commandments,* says:

"There is no word, no hint, in the New Testament about abstaining from work on Sunday. . . . Into the rest of Sunday no divine law enters. . . . The observance of Ash Wednesday or Lent stands on exactly the same footing as the observance of Sunday."—Pages 62, 63, 65.

Reverend Isaac Williams, B.D. (Church of England), in his *Plain Sermons on the Catechism,* says:

"Where are we told in Scripture that we are to keep the first day at all? We are commanded to keep the seventh; but we are nowhere commanded to keep the first day. . . . The reason why we keep the first day of the week holy instead of the seventh is for the same reason that we observe many other things, not because the Bible, but because the church, has enjoined it."—Volume I, pp. 334-336.

William E. Gladstone, England's great prime minister, also of the Church of England, in his *Later Gleanings,* makes these observations:

"The seventh day of the week has been deposed from its title to obligatory religious observance, and its prerogative has been carried over to the first, under no direct precept of Scripture."—Page 342.

In the *Manual of Christian Doctrine* (Protestant Episcopal), this question and answer occur:

"Is there any command in the New Testament to change the day of weekly rest from Saturday to Sunday?—*None.*"— Page 127.

No Scriptural Evidence for the Change

At a New York Ministers' Conference, held November 13, 1893, Dr. Edward T. Hiscox, author of *The Baptist Manual,* read a paper on the transference of the Sabbath from the seventh to the first day. Mention of this paper was made in the November 16, 1893, issue of the New York *Examiner,* a Baptist paper, which described the intense interest manifested by the ministers present, and the discussion that followed its presentation. From a copy of this address, furnished by Dr. Hiscox himself, we call attention to these striking and earnest statements:

"There was and is a commandment to keep holy the Sabbath day, but that Sabbath day was not Sunday. It will be said, however, and with some show of triumph, that the Sabbath was transferred from the seventh to the first day of the week, with all its duties, privileges, and sanctions. Earnestly desiring information on this subject, which I have studied for many years, I ask, Where can the record of such a transaction be found? Not in the New Testament, absolutely not. There is no Scriptural evidence of the change of the Sabbath institution from the seventh to the first day of the week.

"I wish to say that this Sabbath question, in this aspect of it, is the gravest and most perplexing question connected with Christian institutions which at present claims attention from Christian people; and the only reason that it is not a more disturbing element in Christian thought and in religious discussions, is because the Christian world has settled down content on the conviction that somehow a transference has taken place at the beginning of the Christian history. . . .

"To me it seems unaccountable that Jesus, during three years' intercourse with His disciples, often conversing with them upon the Sabbath question, discussing it in some of its various aspects, freeing it from its false glosses, never alluded to any transference of the day; also, that during forty days of His resurrection life, no such thing was intimated. Nor, so far as we know, did the Spirit, which was given to bring to their remembrance all things whatsoever that He had said unto them, deal with this question. Nor yet did the inspired apostles, in preaching the gospel, founding churches, counseling and instructing those founded, discuss or approach this subject.

"Of course, I quite well know that Sunday did come into use in early Christian history as a religious day, as we learn from the Christian Fathers and other sources. But what a pity that it comes branded with the mark of paganism, and christened with the name of the sun god, when adopted and sanctioned by the papal apostasy, and bequeathed as a sacred legacy to Protestantism!"

A Spirit Which Does Not Originate in the Gospel

Dr. H. Gunkel (Lutheran), in *Zum religionsgesch. Verstaendnis des N.T.*, says:

"The taking over of Sunday by the early Christians is, to my mind, an exceedingly important symptom that the early church was directly influenced by a spirit which does not originate in the gospel, nor in the Old Testament, but in a religious system foreign to it."—Page 76.

The Augsburg Confession of Faith (Lutheran) says:

"They [the Catholics] allege the change of the Sabbath into the Lord's day, contrary, as it seemeth, to the decalogue; and they have no example more in their mouths than the change of the Sabbath. They will needs have the church's power to be very great, because it hath dispensed with a precept of the decalogue."—PHILIP SCHAFF, *Creeds of Christendom* (4th ed.), Vol. III, p. 64.

In Binney's *Theological Compend Improved* (Methodist Episcopal), these statements occur:

"It is true there is no positive command for infant baptism. . . . Nor is there any for keeping holy the first day of the week."—Edition of 1902, pp. 180, 181.

No Law in New Testament Regarding First Day

A Theological Dictionary, by Charles Buck (English Independent), says:

"Sabbath in the Hebrew language signifies rest, and is the seventh day of the week, . . . and it must be confessed that there is no law in the New Testament concerning the first day."—Page 403, art. "Sabbath."

In the *Bishop's Pastoral* (Methodist Episcopal) of 1874 this language occurs:

"The Sabbath instituted in the beginning, and confirmed again and again by Moses and the prophets, has never been abrogated. A part of the moral law, not a jot or tittle of its sanctity has been taken away."

Bishop E. O. Haven (Methodist Episcopal), in his *Pillars of Truth,* says:

"The Sabbath was made for man; not for the Hebrews, but for all men."—Page 88.

In *The Works of President Edwards* (Congregationalist) there are these statements regarding the Sabbath:

"A further argument for the perpetuity of the Sabbath we have in Matthew 24:20, 'Pray ye that your flight be not in the winter, neither on the Sabbath day.' Christ is here speaking of the flight of the apostles and other Christians out of Jerusalem and Judea, just before their final destruction, as is manifest by the whole context, and especially by the 16th verse: 'Then let them which be in Judea flee into the mountains.' But the final destruction of Jerusalem was after the dissolution of the Jewish constitution, and after the Christian dispensation was fully set up. Yet it is plainly implied in these words of the Lord, that even then Christians were bound to a strict observation of the Sabbath."—Reprint of Worcester ed., 1844-1848, Vol. IV, pp. 621, 622.

A Universal and Perpetual Obligation

Dr. Archibald Hodge, in Tract No. 175 of the Presbyterian Board of Publication, says:

"God instituted the Sabbath at the creation of man, setting

apart the seventh day for that purpose, and imposed its observance as a universal and perpetual moral obligation upon the race."—Pages 3, 4.

Dr. Thomas Chalmers (Presbyterian) says:

"For the permanency of the Sabbath, however, we might argue its place in the decalogue, where it stands enshrined among the moralities of a rectitude that is immutable and everlasting."—*Sermons,* Vol. I, pp. 51, 52.

Timothy Dwight's *Theology* (Congregationalist) says:

"The Christian Sabbath [Sunday] is not in the Scripture, and was not by the primitive church called the Sabbath."— Sermon 107 (1818 ed.), Vol. IV, p. 49.

Dr. R. W. Dale (Congregationalist), in his *Ten Commandments,* says:

"It is quite clear that, however rigidly or devoutly we may spend Sunday, we are not keeping the Sabbath. . . . The Sabbath was founded on a specific, divine command. We can plead no such command for the obligation to observe Sunday. . . . There is not a single sentence in the New Testament to suggest that we incur any penalty by violating the supposed sanctity of Sunday."—Pages 127-129.

An Embarrassing Situation

But enough of quotations. What shall be said of the anomalous situation in which Protestantism finds itself with regard to Sabbath observance? Here is the church of Christ, called out of Roman Catholicism in the sixteenth century to take its stand on "the Bible and the Bible only," professing loyalty to God's Book, loyalty to God's law, loyalty to God's Sabbath, loyalty to all God's truth, and yet still observing a day that the Bible never once commands to be kept, and altogether discarding the day the Bible declares to be holy.

Depend upon it, the Roman Catholic Church has not failed to observe the embarrassing situation in which its departed daughter finds herself. Perhaps no better comment can be made than the comment by Cardinal Gibbon's official organ, the *Catholic Mirror,* September 23, 1893:

"The Protestant world at its birth [at the beginning of the Reformation in the sixteenth century] found the Christian Sabbath too strongly intrenched to run counter to its existence; it was therefore placed under the necessity of acquiescing in the arrangement, thus implying the church's right to change the day, for over three hundred years. The Christian Sabbath is therefore to this day the acknowledged offspring of the Catholic Church as spouse of the Holy Ghost, without a word of remonstrance from the Protestant world.

"Let us now, however, take a glance at our second proposition, with the Bible alone as the teacher and guide in faith and morals. This teacher most emphatically forbids any change in the day for paramount reasons. The command calls for a 'perpetual covenant.' The day commanded to be kept by the teacher has never once been kept, thereby developing an apostasy from an assumedly fixed principle, as self-contradictory, self-stultifying, and consequently as suicidal as it is within the power of language to express.

"Nor are the limits of demoralization yet reached. Far from it. Their pretense for leaving the bosom of the Catholic Church was for apostasy from the truth as taught in the written Word. They adopted the written Word as their sole teacher, which they had no sooner done than they abandoned it promptly; . . . and by a perversity as willful as erroneous, they accept the teaching of the Catholic Church in direct opposition to the plain, unvaried, and constant teaching of their sole teacher in the most essential doctrine of their religion, thereby emphasizing the situation in what they may be aptly designated 'a mockery, a delusion, and a snare.' "—Reprinted by the Catholic Mirror as a pamphlet, *The Christian Sabbath,* pp. 31, 32.

Of course it is quite impossible for the Sunday observer, who can bring forward no Scripture authority for his disregard of the ancient Sabbath and his reverence for Sunday, to answer the claims of the Catholic Church. But the true Protestant finds no such difficulty, for he denies at once and emphatically the right of any church, however ancient, to change the law of God, and takes his stand squarely and fearlessly upon the written Word. This is his guide, and with him the last source of appeal. Upon this he plants his feet, saying like Luther, "Here I take my stand; I can do no other."

Bible prophecy points to a group of people keeping the true Sabbath down near the end of time and preaching to all men that they should join in thus honoring God's holy day.

Ancient Prophecies of Modern Sabbathkeeping

THE teaching that Christian people today should observe the seventh-day Sabbath is not a new teaching. There are in the Bible prophecies thousands of years old, prophecies with which every Christian should be familiar, that God's people of this age would be Sabbathkeepers.

Peter describes the prophecies of the Bible as "a light that shineth in a dark place" (2 Peter 1:19). These prophecies throw a great volume of light upon the future of the people of God. They make it possible for the student of the Bible to become familiar with the observances of God's people, as they have been foretold in the Scriptures.

Latter-Day Sabbathkeepers

The prophecies of the Old Testament make it plain that in the last days of human history those who are loyal to God will be observers of the seventh-day Sabbath. Thus Isaiah, beholding in heavenly vision the time of the end, the time when "my salvation is near to come, and my righteousness to be revealed" (Isaiah 56:1), cries, "Blessed is the man that doeth this, and the son of man that layeth hold on it; that keepeth the sabbath from polluting it, and keepeth his hand from doing any evil" (verse 2).

This promised blessing for keeping the Sabbath in the days immediately preceding the coming of Christ is not confined to the Jews alone, nor to any one class of people. "Also the sons of the stranger, that join themselves to the Lord, to serve him, and to love the name of the Lord, to be his servants, every one that keepeth the sabbath from polluting it, and taketh hold of my covenant; even them will I bring to my holy mountain, and make them joyful in my house of prayer" (Isaiah 56:6, 7).

In the time of the end, when men are waiting for the coming of Christ, there will be a message of Sabbath reform, a call for those who love Christ to separate themselves from the world and from all opposers, in order to observe the true Sabbath of the Lord and to depart from all sin and evil.

"Shew My People Their Transgression"

At this very time, the time of waiting for the Lord, God commands His messengers: "Cry aloud, spare not, lift up thy voice like a trumpet, and shew my people their *transgression,* and the house of Jacob their sins" (Isaiah 58:1).

In the last days those who profess to be the people of God are to have their attention definitely called to some "transgression" which they are committing. Until their attention is directed to this thing, they are evidently unaware that their practice is wrong in any particular, for God in describing them says, "Yet they seek me daily, and delight to know my ways, as a nation that did righteousness, and forsook not the ordinance of their God: they ask of me the ordinances of justice; they take delight in approaching to God" (Isaiah 58:2).

It is at this time, when those who delight to serve God are unconsciously violating some important requirement of His, when they are forsaking "the ordinance of their God," that

God calls upon His ministers to "cry aloud" and "spare not," to "lift up thy voice like a trumpet, and shew my people their transgression."

The Foundations of Many Generations

God speaks to those who do this work of crying aloud, those who point out the ordinance which His people are forsaking, and says to them: "They that shall be of thee shall build the old waste places: thou shalt raise up the foundations of many generations; and thou shalt be called, The repairer of the breach, The restorer of paths to dwell in" (Isaiah 58: 12).

What the ordinance is which God's professed people in the last days have forsaken is very clearly pointed out in the following verses: "If thou turn away thy foot from [trampling upon] the sabbath, from doing thy pleasure on my holy day; and call the sabbath a delight, the holy of the Lord, honourable; and shalt honour him, not doing thine own ways, nor finding thine own pleasure, nor speaking thine own words: then shalt thou delight thyself in the Lord; and I will cause thee to ride upon the high places of the earth, and feed thee with the heritage of Jacob thy father: for the mouth of the Lord hath spoken it" (Isaiah 58:13, 14).

The "ordinance," then, to which in the last days of the earth's history God's professed people were to be called upon to return, is the fourth precept of the Decalogue, commanding the observance of the Sabbath. This passage in Isaiah points to a time when those who profess to serve the Lord will be trampling the Sabbath under their feet, using it for the performance of their own work and their own pleasure, not giving it the honor due, but calling it "Jewish," and in other ways casting discredit upon it. At this time God calls upon them to cease trampling upon this holy institution, and to call it holy and honorable, not only by word of mouth but by having their lives so cleansed by the blood of Christ that they become true Sabbathkeepers.

This is the important message for today, a message of Sabbath reform. The Lord foresaw the conditions that would prevail in the religious world today, and inspired the prophet to write as he did.

Repairers of the Breach

To those who engage in this work of preaching the truth of the Sabbath question to the world in the last days, God says, "Thou shalt be called, The repairer of the breach, The restorer of paths to dwell in." It will be of interest to notice the significance of these names.

Turning back in the book of Isaiah to the thirtieth chapter, we find disclosed a prophecy that God's professed people in the latter days will be a rebellious people, people who will not hear His law. God calls upon Isaiah to "write it before them in a table, and note it in a book, that it may be for the time to come [margin, "the latter day"] for ever and ever: that this is a rebellious people, lying children, children that will not hear the law of the Lord" (Isaiah 30:8, 9).

A Demand for Smooth Things

These people in the latter days who are rebellious, who will not heed God's law, are in the following verses represented as speaking to their religious leaders, and saying: "Prophesy not unto us right things, speak unto us smooth things, prophesy deceits: get you out of the way, turn aside out of the path, cause the Holy One of Israel to cease from before us" (Isaiah 30:10, 11).

Here is a prophecy that is impossible to misunderstand. It predicts definitely that in the days just before the second coming of Christ, "the latter days," there will be a class of people who profess to serve the Lord, but who are rebellious in the matter of the law, who refuse absolutely to hear or heed the teachings of the law. They will make it plain to their ministers that they do not desire the straight truth, but want "smooth things" preached from the pulpit. They demand of their religious leaders that they shall "turn aside out of the path," and "get out of the way," that they shall speak "smooth things" and "prophesy deceits."

The Path of God's Commandments

What this "path" is, and the "way" here spoken of, will be evident if two or three passages in the Psalms are studied.

"Blessed are the undefiled *in the way, who walk in the law of the Lord*" (Psalm 119:1). "They also do no iniquity: they walk *in his ways*" (verse 3). "Make me to go *in the path of thy commandments;* for therein do I delight" (verse 35).

That the "way" and the "path" spoken of in the prophecy given by Isaiah refer to the law of Ten Commandments will be still further evident from another passage: "Thus saith the Lord, Stand ye in the ways, and see, and ask for the old paths, where is the good way, and walk therein, and ye shall find rest for your souls. But they said, We will not walk therein" (Jeremiah 6:16).

Because His people refuse to walk in the old paths and the good way, God says, "Hear, O earth: behold, I will bring evil upon this people, even the fruit of their thoughts, because they have not hearkened unto my words, nor to my law, but rejected it" (Jeremiah 6:19).

These passages make it clear that the symbols "path" and "way" have reference to the commandments of God, and that to be walking in the way is to be keeping the commandments, and to "turn aside out of the path" is to reject God's law and disobey it.

A Breach in the Law

Returning now to a further study of the remarkable prophecy in Isaiah regarding the last days, and recalling that God predicts that His professed people in these latter days will not hear His law, we now find God likening this rebellion to a breach in a wall.

"Therefore this iniquity shall be to you as a breach ready to fall, swelling out in a high wall, whose breaking cometh suddenly at an instant" (Isaiah 30:13).

Thus the law of God is not only likened to a path and a way in which His people walk but also to a wall that surrounds the trusting Christian and keeps out the attacks of the enemy of his soul. As long as the child of God by the power of Christ stays within the Ten Commandments he is safe from the enemy. The law in Christ is a wall that protects him from being overthrown. As he obeys it he finds it a bulwark against Satan's temptations; but when he disobeys it he has thereby made a breach in his protecting fortress, or wall, and the enemy can come in and overthrow him.

In the last days God saw that a breach would be made in His commandments. One of the commandments would be taken from the ten, leaving a breach, or gap, in the wall. God also foresaw that the religious leaders among His professed people in the last days would not heed His instruction to build up this breach, or gap, by teaching the obligation to observe the seventh-day Sabbath. Moreover, they would actually go so far as to attempt to hide the fact that the breach had been made, and would attempt to cover it up by substituting a false sabbath for the true.

"O Israel, thy prophets are like the foxes in the deserts. Ye have not gone up into the gaps, neither made up the hedge for the house of Israel to stand in the battle in the day of the Lord" (Ezekiel 13:4, 5).

The same subject is here referred to, the same symbols are used, as in the prophecy of Isaiah. The time when these things are to be fulfilled is in the time of preparation for the day of the Lord. The day of the Lord succeeds the day of salvation and refers to the day in which the second coming of Christ will take place.

"The Lord Hath Not Sent Them"

In these days, then, the prophets of God, the ministers, have failed to do what they should have done and what God expected them to do—teach the law of God to their people. To have done this would have meant to prepare their people to stand in the time when all other things are overthrown. But instead of doing this "they have seen vanity and lying divination, saying, The Lord saith: and the Lord hath not sent them: and they have made others to hope that they would confirm the word" (Ezekiel 13:6).

But their "lying divination" in saying that "the Lord saith" is not permitted to stand, for God says to them: "Have ye not seen a vain vision, and have ye not spoken a lying divination, whereas ye say, The Lord saith it; albeit I have not spoken? Therefore thus saith the Lord God; Because ye have spoken vanity, and seen lies, therefore, behold, I am against you, saith the Lord God. And mine hand shall be upon the prophets that see vanity, and that divine lies: they shall not be in the assembly of my people, neither shall they be written in the writing of the house of Israel, neither shall they enter into the land of Israel; and ye shall know that I am the Lord God" (Ezekiel 13:7-9).

"One Built Up a Wall"

The reason is given why they will be thus punished. "Because, even because they have seduced my people, saying, Peace; and there was no peace; and one built up a wall, and, lo, others daubed it with untempered morter" (Ezekiel 13: 10).

Here there is a prediction of an attempt to be made by the religious leaders to cover up the breach which has been made in the law of God. This breach was made by taking out of the law the fourth commandment, the Sabbath commandment.

Now "one" builds up this breach, and "others" try to hide the fact that a false sabbath has been substituted by the "one" for the true Sabbath of Jehovah. They do this by daubing this substitute, or false wall, with "untempered morter" to fill in the breach.

Thus we have here a prophecy that an attempt will be made in the last days to cover up the fact that God's Sabbath has been dishonored by being taken from the law, and another, a false sabbath, put in its place. The "one" who built up the "slight wall" (margin) was the Roman Church. The "others" who "daub it with untempered morter" are the Protestant churches that teach that the change was made with divine sanction and authority. The "untempered morter," with which they attempt to hide the real nature of the counterfeit sabbath, is their saying "The Lord saith" when the Lord has said no such thing.

Foundation to Be Uncovered

The Lord has a special message for those who try to cover up the real facts of the substitution of Sunday for the Sabbath: "Say unto them which daub it with untempered morter, that it shall fall: there shall be an overflowing shower; and ye, O great hailstones, shall fall; and a stormy wind shall rend it. Lo, when the wall is fallen, shall it not be said unto you, Where is the daubing wherewith ye have daubed it? Therefore thus saith the Lord God; I will even rend it with a stormy wind in my fury; and there shall be an overflowing shower in mine anger, and great hailstones in my fury to consume it. So will I break down the wall that ye have daubed with untempered morter, and bring it down to the ground, so that the foundation thereof shall be discovered, and it shall fall, and ye shall be consumed in the midst thereof: and ye shall know that I am the Lord" (Ezekiel 13:11-14).

God is now giving to the world a knowledge of His Sabbath and kindred truths. "This gospel of the kingdom," said Christ, "shall be preached in all the world *for a witness* unto all nations; and then shall the end come." God now says to those who daub their counterfeit wall with untempered mortar, that "it shall fall." The time is coming when God's anger against those who make void His law will no longer sleep. In that day "the foundation" of the Sunday institution "shall be discovered," and "ye, O great hailstones, shall fall." But that day, when God stretches out His hand to punish the inhabitants of the earth for their iniquity, will be when all who will yield their hearts and lives in obedience to Him have done so. The followers of the Lamb will then be made up, and probation closed. (See Isaiah 26:20, 21; Revelation 16:17-21.) The time to learn the truth of the Sabbath question is now, for "now is the accepted time; behold, now is the day of salvation." It is not only important but imperative that we obey God now.

Hiding Their Eyes From the Sabbath

There can be no doubt that it is the Sabbath question with which God is dealing in this figurative way in these prophecies, for, referring again to this same symbol of "untempered morter" in the book of Ezekiel, He says:

"Her priests have violated my law, and have profaned mine holy things: they have put no difference between the holy and profane, neither have they showed difference between the unclean and the clean, *and have hid their eyes from my sabbaths,* and I am profaned among them. Her princes in the midst thereof are like wolves ravening the prey, to shed blood, and to destroy souls, to get dishonest gain. And her prophets have daubed them with untempered morter, seeing vanity, and divining lies unto them, saying, Thus saith the Lord God, when the Lord hath not spoken. . . . And I sought for a man among them, that should make up the hedge, and stand in the gap before me for the land, that I should not destroy it: but I found none" (Ezekiel 22:26-30).

While God finds no one among the religious leaders who will obey Him in making up the hedge and standing in the gap, yet He does find a people through whom He does this work, for He says, "they that shall be of thee shall build the old waste places: thou shalt raise up the foundations of many generations; and thou shalt be called, *The repairer of the breach, The restorer of paths to dwell in"* (Isaiah 58:12).

Thus it is plain from these prophecies that in the last days a people will attempt to restore the Sabbath to its rightful place in the law of God; that they will themselves observe the seventh day for the Sabbath; that they will "cry aloud," and "spare not," and will lift up their voices like trumpets over all the earth to show God's people their transgression; that they will be compelled to meet the bitter opposition of the religious leaders of their time, who will take the side of the Papacy against the truth of God; that they will be acknowledged by the Lord as those who repair the breach made in His law; and that finally, as a result of their faithfulness and constancy, they will ride upon the high places of the earth, and obtain the heritage of Jacob their father, which is the new earth.

Lifting Up a Standard

Another prophecy that undoubtedly refers to this last-day movement to uphold the law is found in Isaiah. "Go through, go through the gates; prepare ye the way of the people; cast up, cast up the highway; gather out the stones; lift up a standard for the people. Behold, the Lord hath proclaimed unto the end of the world, Say ye to the daughter of Zion, Behold thy salvation cometh; behold, his reward is with him, and his work before him" (Isaiah 62:10, 11).

This figure is taken from the ancient custom of removing all obstructions from the path of a king on a visit to another king. A special road was made for him to travel on, the stones were all removed, and a standard bearer preceded him, with a herald to announce his coming.

According to this prophecy something similar to this is to precede the second coming of Christ. There is no doubt that this prophecy relates to the second coming of Christ, for it says He will bring His reward with Him, and He will not do this until He comes the second time (Revelation 22:12). In connection with His coming this prophecy declares that a highway is to be cast up. This we have already seen refers to the path of His commandments. The prophecy also declares that a standard is to be lifted up for the people. This standard is the law of God. It is God's standard of judgment. It was the standard by which God judged Abraham. "Because that Abraham obeyed my voice, and kept my charge, my commandments, my statutes, and my laws" (Genesis 26:5).

It is the standard in which is summed up the whole duty of man. "Let us hear the conclusion of the whole matter: Fear God, and keep his commandments: for this is the whole duty of man" (Ecclesiastes 12:13).

It is the standard by which the human race will be judged. "Whosoever shall keep the whole law, and yet offend in one point, he is guilty of all. For he that said, Do not commit adultery, said also, Do not kill. Now if thou commit no adultery, yet if thou kill, thou art become a transgressor of the law. So speak ye, and so do, as they that shall be judged by the law of liberty" (James 2:10-12).

From these passages, with the prophecy, it is evident that, as a preparation to meet the Lord in peace when He comes the second time, a great message will go to the world, which will emphasize the need of keeping all the Ten Commandments.

The Last Christian Church

This same truth is made plain in the New Testament as well as in the Old. In holy vision the apostle John, on the Isle of Patmos, is permitted to look down through the centuries of the Christian Era. He sees the last Christian church, the church which will meet the Lord at His second coming. And this church John describes. "The dragon was wroth with the woman, and went to make war with the remnant of her seed, *which keep the commandments of God,* and have the testimony of Jesus Christ" (Revelation 12:17).

The "dragon" here represents Satan. The "woman" represents the church of Christ. "The remnant of her seed" has reference to the very end of the church on earth, the church in the days of the second coming of Christ. This church is here pointed out as possessing two marked characteristics: First, it keeps the commandments of God; second, it possesses the gift of prophecy, which is the testimony of Jesus Christ (Revelation 19:10). This last church will be a Sabbathkeeping church, for it never could be truthfully said of any church that did not keep the Sabbath that it kept God's commandments. A church that keeps only nine of God's commandments is a commandment-breaking church. This last church is a commandment-keeping church, a church that keeps the Sabbath.

Again John, looking in vision down through the centuries, sees the last message of the gospel being preached "to every nation, and kindred, and tongue, and people." He describes this message in the fourteenth chapter of Revelation. The message is threefold, and when it is completed, Christ is seen coming in the clouds of heaven to reap the harvest of the earth (Revelation 14:14, 15). Hence this must be the final message to be delivered to mankind. John also sees the people who will deliver the message, and he thus describes them: "Here is the patience of the saints: here are they that keep the commandments of God, and the faith of Jesus" (Revelation 14:12).

So in both the Old and the New Testament God makes it clear to the student of the Bible that every Christian is under obligation to observe every part of His divine law. This law in the last days is to be the test of the faith of His people. And those who stand the test faithfully are given this blessed promise: "Blessed are they that do his commandments, that they may have right to the tree of life, and may enter in through the gates into the city" (Revelation 22:14).

Completing an Arrested Reformation

THE most appalling crisis of its entire history now confronts the Christian church. The faith of the people in the Bible as the inspired and authoritative Word of God is being destroyed not only by attacks from outside the church but by those who occupy positions of foremost trust in its pulpits.

The poisonous influence of modernism, destructive criticism, spiritualism, evolution, and the unwillingness of the ministry of the various churches to accept the plain teachings of the Bible in the place of their sectarian theology, are leading the people away from the great fundamental teachings of the Scriptures, and causing them to place their trust in purely man-made theology.

The drift in the Christian world is away from the simple truths of God's Word. This is due to the fact that there have arisen in the church in recent years many false theories of purely human devising. The tendency of these theories is to lead men to place their confidence and trust for salvation in men, in human effort, in man-made systems, instead of in God, and in the great plan which He has ordained for the salvation of mankind. These false principles and fanciful theories are taking the place, in the minds of the multitude, of the pure gospel of Christ.

These false teachings are sweeping away the faith of the people in the Bible as the word of God. And this attack upon the fundamental truth of Christianity is not, as formerly, from outside the church. The time was when the church was compelled to defend itself from outside antagonists. Infidels, atheists, and agnostics have always found their delight in pointing out what they consider the errors of the Bible, and in laughing at what they term the credulity of the people of God in believing the Scriptures. But they were avowed enemies of the cross of Christ, and it was never a very difficult matter to meet and defeat their attacks.

A New Apostasy

But the situation has changed. Now these enemies of the truth are inside the church, entrenched in positions of great power and influence in the pulpits, the theological seminaries, the great Christian publishing houses. From these points of vantage they are leading a new attack, a most formidable attack, against the Word of God and its inspired teachings.

In reality this is a new apostasy. Sapping its very foundations, poisoning all the springs of its life, these forces are wrecking the church, while at the same time professing to be its friends. Like its divine Master, the Bible—the Word of God—is being "wounded in the house of its friends."

And hence the call today is for a new sounding forth of the ancient truths, a return to the primitive faith of the Bible. The great need of the hour is not only for a Christian faith but also for a Christian experience founded on the Bible and the Bible alone.

During the Dark Ages the truth of the gospel was eclipsed by the darkness and error of false doctrines that had been brought into the church from heathenism. Superstition and ignorance reigned supreme in the hearts of men, crowding out a knowledge of most of the glorious truths of the Bible.

Martin Luther was the most prominent among those who were called of God to lead the world out of the darkness of a false system of religion into a purer faith. He was devoted, ardent, zealous. He knew no fear but the fear of God, and acknowledged no foundation for religious faith but the Holy Scriptures. He was pre-eminently the man for his time. Through this man and his faithful associates God accomplished a great work for the reformation of the church and the enlightenment of the world.

The Progress of Reform

But God did not reveal all His truth to Luther. He designed that the Reformation should be a progressive work, that men should hold their minds open in their search of the Scriptures and be ready always to accept such new light as in His providence He should send them. And yet when Luther died, those who had been associated with him did not go on to learn the whole truth of God. His followers gathered together what he had believed, and out of it made a creed. They settled themselves down upon that creed as if they had advanced as far as possible in the knowledge of truth.

God had other truths to reveal to the world, but by adopting a creed based upon Luther's belief, the followers of Luther made it impossible for God to send more truth to the world through them. When people refuse to accept anything more than is contained in their creed, they shut themselves away from new light by refusing to go beyond what their creed already contains.

Similarly God called other men to advance the work of the Reformation. He called Knox and Calvin, and through them He did a great work in making known the principles of the gospel. That work should have continued to grow. The adherents of truth should have studied the Bible constantly, thus coming to the knowledge of more and more truth, and preaching it to the world. Instead of doing this, they made the same mistake that had been made before. Other denominations were formed. Creeds were constructed out of the teachings of Knox and Calvin, and its adherents settled down on that creed as if that were the sum of all truth.

God caused still other men to advance the cause of His truth. He purposed to reveal to the world the truth in all its fullness, and sought for men through whom this could be done. Reformers arose likewise in England. But while they renounced some of the errors of Rome, they retained many of her forms. Thus while the authority and creed of the Roman church were rejected, not a few of her customs and ceremonies became incorporated into the worship of the Church of England.

"A Misery Much to Be Lamented"

God gave the Pilgrim Fathers more light and truth, and also the Puritans. They earnestly desired to return to the simplicity and purity of the apostolic church, but they were persecuted and driven out of England, and came to America. That some among them plainly discerned the right attitude all men should assume toward the truth is evident from the statements contained in the farewell address of one of their pastors, John Robinson, delivered on the shore of Holland when the Pilgrims were about to depart for America. John Robinson said:

"Brethren, we are now ere long to part asunder, and the Lord knoweth whether I shall live ever to see your faces more.

But whether the Lord hath appointed it or not, I charge you before God and His blessed angels to follow me no farther than I have followed Christ. If God should reveal anything to you by any other instrument of His, be as ready to receive it as ever you were to receive any truth of my ministry, for I am very confident the Lord hath more truth and light yet to break forth out of His holy Word."—W. CARLOS MARTYN, *The Pilgrim Fathers of New England* (1867), p. 70.

"For my part, I cannot sufficiently bewail the condition of the Reformed churches, who are come to a period of religion, and will go at present no farther than the instruments of their reformation. The Lutherans cannot be drawn to go beyond what Luther saw, . . . and the Calvinists, you see, stick fast where they were left by that great man of God, who yet saw not all things. This is a misery much to be lamented, for though they were burning and shining lights in their times, yet they penetrated not into the whole counsel of God, but were they now living, would be as willing to embrace further light as that which they first received."—DANIEL NEAL, *History of the Puritans* (1848), Vol. I, pp. 269, 270.

"Remember your church covenant, in which you have agreed to walk in all the ways of the Lord, made or to be made known unto you. Remember your promise and covenant with God and with one another to receive whatever light and truth shall be made known to you from His written Word; but withal, take heed, I beseech you, what you receive for truth, and compare it and weigh it with other scriptures of truth before you accept it; for it is not possible the Christian world should come so lately out of such thick antichristian darkness, and that full perfection of knowledge should break forth at once."—*The Pilgrim Fathers of New England,* pp. 70, 71.

This certainly was excellent counsel, and should have

been carefully heeded and conscientiously obeyed, as it was indeed by the Pilgrims at Plymouth for a while. But no sooner had the Puritans become established at Massachusetts Bay in the New World than they violated all the principles of Christianity and Protestantism by creating a theocracy, and going into the business of persecuting dissenters. They themselves would not advance beyond their man-made creed; neither would they permit anyone else to do so.

Advancement of Truth Retarded

The Wesleys were called of God and did a mighty gospel work. But God had still more truth to reveal to the world. When men accepted only certain truths, and of these made creeds, refusing to receive more truth than that contained within narrow creedal limits, they shut themselves away from God; they limited the Holy One of Israel. Wesley's followers made the same mistake as those who had preceded them, selecting a few of the many truths God had for the world, reducing these to a written creed, and thus excluding additional light from Heaven. Hence it was inevitable that God should choose faithful, honest souls who would give the world not only the truths the Wesleys preached but also the additional light revealed of God.

One of the most solemn and yet most glorious truths revealed in the Bible is that of the second coming of Christ to this earth to complete the great work of redemption. This truth is the very keynote of the Sacred Scriptures, for it is the consummation of all the hopes of the Christian church.

The time was drawing near when this great truth should be preached to the world. It was the purpose of God to reveal this doctrine to, and have it preached by, those whom He had called to be leaders in the work of reformation. But by their

I

THOU SHALT HAVE NO OTHER GODS BEFORE ME.

II

THOU SHALT NOT MAKE UNTO THEE ANY GRAVEN IMAGE, OR ANY LIKENESS OF ANY THING THAT IS IN HEAVEN ABOVE, OR THAT IS IN THE EARTH BENEATH, OR THAT IS IN THE WATER UNDER THE EARTH: THOU SHALT NOT BOW DOWN THY-SELF TO THEM, NOR SERVE THEM: FOR I THE LORD THY GOD AM A JEALOUS GOD, VISITING THE INIQUITY OF THE FATHERS UPON THE CHILDREN UNTO THE THIRD AND FOURTH GENERATION OF THEM THAT HATE ME; AND SHEWING MERCY UNTO THOUSANDS OF THEM THAT LOVE ME, AND KEEP MY COMMANDMENTS.

III

THOU SHALT NOT TAKE THE NAME OF THE LORD THY GOD IN VAIN; FOR THE LORD WILL NOT HOLD HIM GUILTLESS THAT TAKETH HIS NAME IN VAIN.

IV

REMEMBER THE SABBATH DAY, TO KEEP IT HOLY. SIX DAYS SHALT THOU LABOUR, AND DO ALL THY WORK: BUT THE SEVENTH DAY IS THE SABBATH OF THE LORD THY GOD: IN IT THOU SHALT NOT DO ANY WORK, THOU, NOR THY SON, NOR THY DAUGHTER, THY MANSERVANT, NOR THY MAID-SERVANT, NOR THY CATTLE, NOR THY STRANGER THAT IS WITHIN THY GATES: FOR IN SIX DAYS THE LORD MADE HEAVEN AND EARTH, THE SEA, AND ALL THAT IN THEM IS, AND RESTED THE SEVENTH DAY: WHEREFORE THE LORD BLESSED THE SABBATH DAY, AND HALLOWED IT.

V

HONOUR THY FATHER AND THY MOTHER: THAT THY DAYS MAY BE LONG UPON THE LAND WHICH THE LORD THY GOD GIVETH THEE.

VI

THOU SHALT NOT KILL.

VII

THOU SHALT NOT COMMIT ADULTERY.

VIII

THOU SHALT NOT STEAL.

IX

THOU SHALT NOT BEAR FALSE WITNESS AGAINST THY NEIGHBOUR.

X

THOU SHALT NOT COVET THY NEIGHBOUR'S HOUSE, THOU SHALT NOT COVET THY NEIGHBOUR'S WIFE, NOR HIS MANSERVANT, NOR HIS MAID-SERVANT, NOR HIS OX, NOR HIS ASS, NOR ANY THING THAT IS THY NEIGHBOUR'S.

Today the special message in regard to God's holy Sabbath is being preached far and wide, calling upon men in every land and every station of life to adjust their lives to God's commands.

course they had shut themselves away from this new truth. Therefore, when the time came to have the message of His coming preached in all the world, He found it necessary again to go outside of the established churches and initiate another movement that would take to the ends of the earth the proclamation of Christ's second coming.

Along with the message of His coming, God designed that all the truths that had been falsified and hidden during the Dark Ages should again be made clear to the human family, so that at His coming the fullness of the truth might be revealed to the world. Many of the Protestant bodies, in severing themselves from Rome, had brought along with them some of the errors of Rome.

Restoration of the Sabbath

Among these errors was the keeping of the first day of the week in place of the true Sabbath of God, which is the seventh day. The observance of the Sabbath had been changed by the Church of Rome, and many Protestants, not having investigated its origin, accepted it with other things that they had not studied. In the last message God designed to send to the human family immediately preceding His return to this earth, the confusion concerning this question was to be cleared up, and the true Sabbath of God restored to its rightful place in the gospel and in the hearts of God's people.

Hence, in addition to containing the truth of the second coming of Christ, God's final message will also contain the truth on the Sabbath question. When this is preached to the people of the earth, they are under the same obligation to accept it and bring their lives into harmony with it as were the men of Luther's day under obligation to walk in the light God caused to shine upon their pathway.

Among other errors which have been brought out of the Church of Rome into some of the Protestant churches are the teachings concerning eternal torment, infant baptism, and sprinkling for baptism. None of these have a foundation in the teachings of the Bible. In this last message which is to go to all the earth all errors must be discarded by those who would receive from God the truth in its fullness.

Hence it can be seen that the message of the second coming of Christ and the keeping of the commandments of God is not only the final message of the gospel, but it is also the completion of the Reformation of the sixteenth century, which has heretofore been retarded and arrested by the formation of denominational creeds.

It is of vital importance to all Christians that they guard against being bound by a written creed, however perfect it may seem to be. There is still more light to break forth from the Bible, and when God reveals it to us, we should be in an attitude of mind that will make it possible to accept it. Christians should have no other creed but the blessed Bible itself. Faith should be built on that, and if it is discovered that we are believing anything which cannot be substantiated by the teachings of the Bible, that belief should at once be discarded. The Bible and the Bible alone should be the basis of the religion of Christians.

In this time when men of great learning and high position in the churches are endeavoring to prove that the Bible is not true, it is important that the man of faith fortify himself with the protection to be found in the truth of the Bible. Study the Bible earnestly, search it diligently, and let its blessed principles become incorporated into the life.

"Take unto you the whole armour of God, that ye may be able to withstand in the evil day, and having done all, to stand.

Stand therefore, having your loins girt about with truth, and having on the breastplate of righteousness; and your feet shod with the preparation of the gospel of peace; above all, taking the shield of faith, wherewith ye shall be able to quench all the fiery darts of the wicked. And take the helmet of salvation, and the sword of the Spirit, which is the word of God: praying always with all prayer and supplication in the Spirit, and watching thereunto with all perseverance and supplication for all saints" (Ephesians 6:13-18).

Only those who have fortified their minds with the great truths of the Bible will stand during the trying time just ahead.

Walking
in the Light

THERE is no higher duty for any rational being than to learn from the Scriptures what is truth. Day by day the Bible should be studied diligently. Every thought that presents itself to the mind should be carefully weighed, and scripture should be compared with scripture. In this way, with the aid of God's Spirit, we should form our opinions for ourselves, for it must ever be remembered that we are to answer for ourselves before God.

As the Word of God is thus studied, a knowledge of the truth will be imparted. Searching the Scriptures will lead, step by step, into all truth. As the light of truth comes, it should be followed. Only so will more truth be given. As men walk in the light they have, more light will be given. They cannot expect to be guided by God's Spirit unless they follow all the way. There can never come a time in Christian experience when it will be right to draw back as truth is revealed through the Word of God by His Spirit. The light will become darkness if men refuse to walk in it.

God will send more and more light to His people until the end of time. Breaking forth from the Bible constantly will come new truths, truths that are not contained in the creeds of the churches. So it has always been. Luther was called of God to accept new light, and he did so, and the result was the great Reformation of the sixteenth century. So Calvin and Knox and Wesley found new light, and they walked in it.

A Message Containing Advanced Truth

And now, in this day, God has sent a message to all the world, a warning of the nearness of the second coming of Christ. In that message is contained new light. It is truth for this time, and all who hear the message are called upon to accept it.

In this message is new light on the Sabbath question, the nature of man, the state of the dead, the reward of the righteous, the fate of the wicked, and the millennium. A great conflict between truth and error is just before us, the closing struggle of the age-long controversy between sin and righteousness. Only those who have fortified their minds with the great truths of the Bible will stand through the trying times just ahead. To every soul will come the searching test, Shall I obey God rather than man? Indeed, we are even now in that decisive hour. Where do you stand? Are your feet planted on the solid rock, the Word of God? Are you unyielding in defense of the commandments of God and the faith of Jesus?

To follow the plain teachings of the Bible in this "progressive age" is considered by many, even by some religious teachers, to be old-fashioned and inconvenient. It is not for them to hear and follow the teachings of the Saviour; they prefer to subscribe to a more liberal creed.

Reluctance to Investigate Truth

The pure religion of Christ is being obscured by cold formality and by the power of a creed. We are informed that the present age is one of great liberality in religious matters, and that the truly pious are taking on great breadth of mind. Thus tens of thousands of people are allowing their preachers to do their thinking for them. The result is that there are multitudes who can give no reason for the things they believe other than that they were so taught by their pastor. The beaten track is well traveled, there being many who are reluctant to step aside and make an independent investigation of the truth. Many are content to follow in the steps of learned men; hesitating to investigate truth for themselves, they are held fast in error's chains.

Truth has come into the world, but men love darkness rather than light. They are following the way of error, and they love to have it so. If the disciples of Christ were to return today and come teaching in our cities as poverty-stricken and hungry as they were when they taught on the hills of Galilee, and should visit some of the magnificent churches that are called by the names of these very disciples, where the worshipers sit clothed in their purple and fine linen, and the modern Pharisee makes himself prominent by his cold "God, I thank Thee that I am not as other men," they would not be permitted to present their message of truth until they had first been questioned as to denominational affiliation and submitted to an examination in which they would be required to give their assent to doctrines and creeds of which they had never before heard.

Darkness May Replace Light

"Yet a little while is the light with you. Walk while ye have the light, lest darkness come upon you: for he that walketh in darkness knoweth not whither he goeth. While ye have light, believe in the light, that ye may be the children of light" (John 12:35, 36).

The rejection of light, of truth, causes men to walk in darkness, in error. Many hear God's final message. Some accept it, others reject it. The result of rejection will be that darkness will take the place of light, "and he that walketh in darkness knoweth not whither he goeth."

The wise man said, "The path of the just is as the shining light, that shineth more and more unto the perfect day" (Proverbs 4:18).

More and more light will shine upon the pathway of the child of God until the day of Christ's appearing. As light comes, it is our duty to walk in it. That is the solemn obligation resting upon every person who becomes acquainted with God's final message for the last days.

It is just as true today that men love darkness rather than light as it was when Jesus spoke it. Just as in His day there was brought to the people the truthful message of His first coming, so today there is going to the world the true message of His second coming. Today it is true that "light is come into the world, and men loved darkness rather than light." It is not necessary to commit some gross sin to be lost. A refusal to follow Christ, to walk in the light, will surely result in the utter loss of the soul. Let it not be true of anyone who reads these words that he loves darkness rather than light. On the contrary, when you see and hear and are convicted of the truth of God's great final message, accept it with a glad heart, bringing your life into conformity with it.

Light in the Bible

"Thy word is a lamp unto my feet, and a light unto my path" (Psalm 119:105). "The entrance of thy words giveth light; it giveth understanding unto the simple" (verse 130).

Thus anything clearly taught in the Bible is light, and

must be accepted by the people of God if they are to walk therein.

Light in the Law

"The commandment is a lamp; and the law is light; and reproofs of instruction are the way of life" (Proverbs 6:23).

Whatever is taught in the law of God and the Word of God, as this message is which you have been reading, should be followed and received into the heart. Not to accept this message would be to reject light and truth, and no Christian can afford to do that.

Light in the Prophecies

"We have also a more sure word of prophecy; whereunto ye do well that ye take heed, as unto a light that shineth in a dark place, until the day dawn, and the day star arise in your hearts" (2 Peter 1:19).

Here prophecy is called a light. As prophecy, then, is fulfilled and its meaning unfolds, it is obvious that there will be laid upon men the constant obligation of following and accepting such new truths as it shall disclose.

Inasmuch as prophecy, according to Daniel 12:4, is to be understood in "the time of the end," it is plain that in this time the attention of men will be directed to new light, new truth. Daniel's prophecies are unfolding, they are being fulfilled, and we see their meaning. This lays upon us the obligation of walking in the light they contain.

The prophecies of Revelation are also being fulfilled today. God has thus spoken of them: "Blessed is he that readeth, and they that hear the words of this prophecy, and keep those things which are written therein" (Revelation 1:3).

From this it is plain that as Bible prophecy unfolds there is to be a continual revelation of new duties, which must be obeyed by God's people.

Fullness of Light in the Threefold Message

In the book of Revelation is the prophecy of the great threefold message that will close the work of the gospel (Revelation 14:6-12). This message contains a revelation of new duties. It is based on God's Word, God's law, and the prophecies of the Bible. It contains the truth of heaven for the present time. It is going to all the world in this generation, and when this work is completed, the end of all things earthly will come.

In this "everlasting gospel" is salvation for those who accept it, and in it also is an abundant entrance into the kingdom of God. "Blessed are they that do his commandments, that they may have right to the tree of life, and may enter in through the gates into the city" (Revelation 22:14).

Those who accept this last message, who lay hold upon "the faith of Jesus," and through faith keep His commandments, will enter into the city of God. It is our privilege as well as our duty to investigate the truth for this time, and when we learn that it is truth, to accept it and obey it.

> "O that our thoughts and thanks may rise
> As grateful incense to the skies,
> And draw from Christ that sweet repose
> Which none but he who feels it knows.

> "This heavenly calm within the breast
> Is the best pledge of glorious rest,
> Which for the church of God remains,
> The end of cares, the end of pains."